Praise for: *Freedom from addiction*

"Following *How to Lift Depression...fast*
recommended. It sidesteps jargon, avoids the medicalisation of
addictive behaviour, explodes the lies that maintain addiction and
offers realistic, practical solutions." *Nursing Standard*

"So many books promise so much, and then fail to deliver. This book
is of an entirely different quality. If you have an addiction/compulsive
behaviour, do yourself a big favour, buy it – it gives answers ... a big
thank you to the authors." *Amazon Review*

"An easy-to-read, empowering self-help guide for those considering
themselves 'addicted' to anything... It breaks down simply the self-
assessment needed for discerning problem areas and their development, adding relevant research in a jargon-free manner; with a fascin-
ng explanation for how neurophysiology and 'pattern-matching'
underpin symptoms like craving." *Neia Glynn, The Psychologist*

"Full of insights, this book is truly superb, not just in the area of understanding and managing addictions but also in providing a broader,
clear, coherent and wholly convincing insight into human thought
processes and behaviours. A great book, even if you don't suffer from,
or work professionally with, addictive behaviour." *Amazon Review*

"Here is another excellent book from that groundbreaking team, Joe
Griffin and Ivan Tyrrell. This time the focus is on addiction, how it
comes about, and a highly effective way of dealing with it – whether it
is a life threatening addiction (and many are) or an annoying habit
which one would like to be rid of... There are techniques and ways of
looking at problems which we can assimilate and pass on to our
clients. *Freedom from Addiction* is easy to read, gives clear guidance
and is an ideal book to have to hand to enable you to help yourself,
your family, your friends and your clients." *Ruth Morozzo*

"I purchased this book primarily to help me stop smoking. After a
one day read I applied the principles in it and have not had a cigarette
for three weeks. *Freedom from Addiction* is amazing in that it takes you
through the chemical process behind addiction and reveals the tricks
the mind plays to trap one into performing addictive behaviours. The
advice contained in it for defusing the addictive process and handling
cravings is first class. It also contains information on human needs and
the tools nature has provided one with to meet them. The authors
explore these needs in depth and this explanation of the way things
are meant to work makes it easier to see how things go wrong. I fully
recommend this book." *Amazon Review*

The Human Givens Approach Series is a range of best-selling books, each of which explores a recognised psychological or behavioural problem and shows in clear, non-jargonistic language how to treat it effectively with psychological interventions.

Freedom from Addiction is the second title in the series, which includes *How to lift depression – fast; How to Master Anxiety: All you need to overcome stress, panic attacks, phobias, trauma, obsessions and more; Release from Anger: Practical help for controlling unreasonable rage* and *How to Liberate yourself from Pain: Practical help for sufferers.* (The series is part of a larger nationwide effort to move counselling, psychotherapy and education away from ideology and more into line with scientific findings about how the brain works and what people really need to live fulfilling lives.)

Joe Griffin is a research psychologist with graduate and postgraduate degrees from the LSE. He is hugely influential in the world of psychotherapy and is a director of the Human Givens Institute. He is co-author with Ivan Tyrrell of *How to lift depression – fast; How to Master Anxiety; Release from Anger; Dreaming Reality: How dreaming keeps us sane or can drive us mad; Human Givens: A new approach to emotional health and clear thinking* and *Godhead: The brain's big bang.*

Ivan Tyrrell has worked for many years as a psychotherapist and now spends most of his time lecturing and writing. For fourteen years he was Principal of Mindfields College, and is now Director of Human Givens College, which teaches a wide-range of psychotherapeutic skills to health and welfare professionals across the UK. He is Editorial Director of the *Human Givens* journal and a director of the Human Givens Institute. As a result, his influence (and knowledge of) the field of psychotherapy and counselling is considerable.

Denise Winn is a journalist specialising in psychology and medicine, and editor of the *Human Givens* journal.

Freedom from
addiction

The secret behind successful
addiction busting

Change is much easier
than you think...

Joe Griffin & Ivan Tyrrell

with Denise Winn

ALSO BY THE AUTHORS

Godhead: The brain's big bang
Joe Griffin and Ivan Tyrrell

*Human Givens: A new approach to
emotional health and clear thinking*
Joe Griffin and Ivan Tyrrell

*Dreaming Reality: How dreaming
keeps us sane or can drive us mad*
Joe Griffin and Ivan Tyrrell

How to lift depression – fast
Joe Griffin and Ivan Tyrrell

How to Master Anxiety
Joe Griffin and Ivan Tyrrell

Release from Anger
Joe Griffin and Ivan Tyrrell

*An Idea in Practice: Using the
human givens approach*
Joe Griffin and Ivan Tyrrell (Eds)

The Origin of Dreams
Joe Griffin

The Survival Option
Ivan Tyrrell

Freedom from
addiction

The secret behind successful
addiction busting

A practical handbook

PUBLISHING

Joe Griffin & Ivan Tyrrell

with Denise Winn

PUBLISHING

First published in Great Britain 2005
Reprinted 2006, 2008, 2012

Published by HG Publishing, an imprint of Human Givens Publishing Ltd,
Chalvington, East Sussex, BN27 3TD, United Kingdom.
www.humangivens.com

A catalogue record for this book is available from the British Library.

ISBN-10: 1 899398 46 5
ISBN-13: 978 1 899398 46 1

Typeset in Book Antiqua and Conduit Condensed.
Printed and bound by CPI Group (UK) Ltd, Croydon, CR0 4YY.
Index by Indexing Specialists (UK) Ltd.

*"The greatest wealth is a
poverty of desires."*

SENECA

CONTENTS

Acknowledgements

We would like to thank our many patients, friends
and colleagues for helping us in the research for this
book, and our editor, Jane Tyrrell, for helping
us bring clarity of expression to
the ideas it contains.

There's nothing as certain as change

*I*F YOU are becoming worried about an aspect of your own behaviour – maybe you no longer feel totally in control of it, or are concerned about the health implications, or the fact that it takes up so much of your time and money – and you've decided that you want to do something about it, this book will help you.

You might not think of yourself as having an addiction. Perhaps you prefer to call the behaviour you're worried about a compulsion or a dependence, a craving, or simply a bit of fun – it doesn't really matter what term you use to describe it. What *does* matter, however, is that you have at least the stirrings of concern about it, certainly enough to lead you to open this book (whether or not you picked it up yourself or it was given to you by someone else). The important thing to remember is that anyone can overcome addiction, if they truly want to – and the first step is the one you have already taken, however tentatively.

And you are not alone. Many people are caught up in self-destructive compulsive behaviours that they wish they could stop or dramatically reduce. Some we have figures for – the number who smoke, take drugs or drink to excess and the numbers who die from smoking, drug- and drink-related diseases each year. For many, though, we don't have figures – or else we only have rough estimates: the numbers of people who work compulsively, eat compulsively, shop compulsively, have sex compulsively, self-harm compulsively, study compulsively, have plastic surgery compulsively and a multitude of other activities. In fact anything pleasurable (even if it might not be an obvious candidate for addiction) can become addictive if it is done compulsively in the desperate search for a lift of mood. We can as easily become addicted to attention, possessions, power, money and excitement as to drink, food, mood-altering drugs and so on.

But why is it that we can become addicted to so many different, and sometimes strange, things? Why should someone become addicted to risking life and limb through extreme sports, say, or risk ruining their life and perhaps losing their family because of gambling? And why do so many of us continue to smoke or drink heavily, despite the effect we know it has on our health? Indeed, why would nature – which designed us to survive and thrive – allow such a potentially destructive vulnerability to evolve?

The answers provide us with the elusive key to successful addiction busting.

This book is different!

This book presents you with some exciting new understandings about addiction – understandings that will not only give you a completely fresh outlook on why you do what it is you do excessively but also make it much easier for you to take back control of that behaviour.

It has only recently been recognised that all addictive behaviours – whether smoking, drinking, shopaholism, workaholism, gambling, watching too much TV, seeking too much sex, taking too much exercise, buying books you don't read, or any of a host of others – work through the same common pathways in the brain – the *'expectation'* pathway. By understanding and acting on this new knowledge you can stop addictive behaviour in its tracks – and also break the common pattern of switching from one addictive behaviour to another.

If you absorb the information in this book – and it is not difficult – you will see how you can use your own natural abilities to defeat addiction and create a more satisfying life for yourself. This is the human givens approach to beating addictive behaviour that works *with* the givens of human nature, rather than trying to thwart them, as so many other methods unsuccessfully try to do. It is similar, in principle, to the way a judo master uses his opponent's own strength to overcome him.

You don't need a book about your own specific addiction

Although it might seem strange, you don't actually need a book that focuses exclusively on one form of addiction. Rather, you need to understand the common pattern that lies behind *all* addictions. (But there is also plenty of information within these pages that relates to specific addictions.) If you let yourself truly take on board the information offered in this book, you can apply it to absolutely any addictive activity. And you'll find 'giving up' much easier than you could ever have imagined.

> 66 We need to understand the common pattern that lies behind *all* addictions. 99

PLEASE NOTE: To protect confidentiality, the biographical details in the case histories used in this book have been changed.

PART 1

Understanding addiction

$\mathscr{P}$ERHAPS you have tried before to stop or cut back the compulsive activity you now want to learn to control or cut out completely. You start the first day, determined, full of hope. Perhaps you've even decided to do lots of healthy activities instead of *that* one, planning to go for a walk or clean out a cupboard, to keep your mind off it, or to drink plenty of water or orange juice and eat raw carrot sticks, so as to feel healthy and ready for a fresh start. At first everything is fine. But then you arrive at a certain time of day or are in a particular place or doing a particular thing or feeling a certain way that makes you think of it, and makes you want to do it, have it, go there now – whatever 'it' may be for you.

You push the desire away. But it is insistent. It keeps coming back. You feel it strongly, perhaps literally, in the form of a wanting sensation in your mouth or your stomach or dizziness in your head. You start to feel you can't go on without it; life is worthless; nothing will ever be fun or exciting again. You tell yourself off for being ridiculous. After all, other people do without it. They don't even *want* to do it. Yet you can't pull your mind away from it.

Perhaps you manage to overcome the temptation once, twice, ten times. But you don't feel triumphant. You feel obsessed by the urge you are struggling against and are desperate just to get through the day, to get to bedtime and oblivion. With the new day, perhaps you feel new hope for a while, or maybe the misery gets right out of bed with you. Whichever, you sink deeper into gloom and the desperation gets stronger and stronger. Sooner or later, you give in.

Or maybe you have never tried to stop or cut down. When you think about your habit, you feel a flicker of fear, a moment of numbness – you don't want to ruin your health and the lives of those you love – but you push the thought away. It's too frightening to go there. You comfort yourself that you'll deal with it, one day. Just, not yet. Because getting to grips with it now, and all the pain that will entail, is just too agonising to contemplate.

Or perhaps you have no trouble giving up. For the first month or two or four, it's as if it was never a problem at all. But then something happens, or you are in a certain place, or you feel a certain feeling and, before you know it, you have indulged again. There's a rush of the expected pleasure but it is dwarfed by the accompanying rush of guilt and disbelief, self-loathing and hopelessness. You were doing so well. Why, you demand of yourself, does it always have to end up like this, as if you have no control over the habit at all?

Well, it *doesn't* have to be like any of that – or any other miserable experience you associate with trying to give up whatever unhealthy, habitual activity bothers you.

The first step towards making it different this time is to understand *why* you feel the way you do, and *what* you can do, quite simply, to change it. In Part 2, we'll get on to *how*.

Understanding what drives your addictive behaviour is an important part of the process of getting it under control. This book gives you some new ideas about why it is in all of our natures to be vulnerable to addiction. And, most importantly, how this knowledge can help us handle addictions in a healthy way.

Whenever we explain these ideas in our seminars and therapy sessions, people tell us that it's as if a 'light' has been switched on in their brains and, by

> 66 Understanding what drives your addictive behaviour is an important part of getting it under control. 99

seeing how and why they have become addicted, they are then able to begin taking the necessary steps to beat their addiction. So, as you can see, the information in this section is very important for you to read and digest.

Whether you are desperate to stop your compulsive activity or are simply at the stage where you just have niggling concerns about it – but concerns that you find difficult to push away – read on. (However, if someone has thrust this book upon you but you yourself still feel quite happy about your addictive activity, leave it aside until those niggling concerns do start to surface.)

But do I actually have an addiction?

An addiction is a habitual indulgence in any substance, activity or practice that is beyond your control and affects your life for the worse.

Some people, even those who smoke 40 cigarettes a day or drink 12 pints of beer a night, resist the idea that they have an 'addiction'. The word is too closely connected to 'addict', with

> 66 When I'm on the internet, in chatrooms, I feel full of confidence. I can be the person I want to be and my words come out right. I feel powerful, instead of a shy, spotty teenager who stammers. That's why I spend every moment I can online. 99
> 14-YEAR-OLD BOY

> 66 I crave sugar. 99
> 44-YEAR-OLD WOMAN

> 66 When I'm upset, I eat. I just have to go for the fridge. I can't keep my mind off food and yet, when I'm eating, it's so fast and I feel so guilty that I don't even taste it." 99
> 24-YEAR-OLD WOMAN

> 66 I get a lot of backache because of my job, so having a drink is like a bit of anaesthetic, really. I always mean just to have one or two, to kill the pain, but then I get into it and don't stop. The trouble is my wife is now threatening to divorce me because I get violent, sometimes, when I'm drunk. 99
> 35-YEAR-OLD MAN

> 66 I earn a lot for someone my age and I work hard for it, so I don't have time for relationships. My buzz is going shopping and buying whatever I want. I don't feel guilty about it, although I suppose it would be nice to have someone to wear the clothes for. 99
> 30-YEAR-OLD WOMAN

> 66 I hate smoking. I smoke 40 a day and only ever enjoy the first one of the morning. So why on earth can't I stop? 99 52-YEAR-OLD MAN

all the negative connotations that that word carries. But, as we have said, it doesn't really matter what word you use. It is the behaviour associated with the addiction, dependence, habit or craving – whatever you want to call it – that tells you whether you have a problem. Have a look at the following questions to see if your behaviour is out of your control.

1. Do you spend a lot of time on your problem activity?

Give this some thought, and you might be surprised by just how much time your compulsive activity takes up in one way or another. For instance, people who drink to excess typically spend time getting to the particular pub or club that they like to drink in or going to buy alcohol to take home. They will spend several hours engaged in drinking in one setting or another and then, perhaps, several more hours getting over the after-effects of sickness or hangover. People addicted to illegal drugs must often spend time finding ways to acquire the large sums of money required to feed their habit – resorting perhaps even to theft or prostitution – as well as the time spent going to buy the drug and then taking it. People who shop to excess must take the time to go to the shops (or surfing internet shopping sites) and perhaps spend a considerable amount of time making their choices. For those who have a compulsion for sex, much time may be spent hanging around in places where potential partners can be met, as well as in the sexual encounters themselves. Workaholics, by the very nature of their addiction, must spend inordinately long hours performing their jobs. People addicted to power devote years to manipulating other people to get it. Compulsive TV-watching or computer game playing eats up the hours, and so on.

> **Obsessive preoccupation is experienced with any addictive behaviour.**

Even smoking, which seemingly can be done alongside everyday activities, also takes up considerable time – time spent buying cigarettes, perhaps rolling them, finding where the packet or the lighter has been left, making one's way to a designated smoking area at work, or outside the building (because there is no designated area any more), making unintended trips to the shops or the petrol station because cigarettes have run out, and so on.

All of these addictive behaviours, and the countless others we haven't mentioned, are very different from each other, yet they all eat into people's time. And they all have something else very important in common too, which is:

> *Anyone with an addictive behaviour spends*
> *a great deal of time thinking about it!*

Thinking about your problem activity

You may not be conscious of it, but you *are* doing it. For instance, if you drink that bit too heavily, you will probably think about when you can get your first drink of the day, or you might spend time looking forward to your next opportunity for a binge-drinking session. And, if you are prevented by other duties or responsibilities from taking a drink, you will be thinking about how much you want one. You may also spend a lot of time thinking about how you wish you didn't drink so much and resolving that tomorrow will be different. Likewise, people who overeat or undereat commonly find themselves thinking about food. Even if they are not planning to eat the food themselves, they may spend inordinate amounts of time thinking about what they will cook for other people.

Warning!

YOU MAY be addicted to prescription drugs, such as tranquillisers, antidepressants or migraine medication, if you need to keep upping your dosage in order to get an effect or to control increasingly frequent symptoms. **Do not stop taking such drugs without consulting your GP.** It is very likely that you will need to withdraw slowly, to prevent or minimise discontinuation effects caused by the drug. Your GP can advise you how to do this safely.

Such obsessive preoccupation is experienced with any addictive behaviour.

Here are a few more examples. People who exercise too much must plan their visits to the gym or their runs in the park. As they exercise, and even when they aren't, they may be thinking about whether they are working hard enough, performing well enough, etc. They may think that they need to increase the amount, or vary the type, of exercise that they do and worry about how to fit the extra load into their day, or about the fact that they don't actually have the time to do more.

Smokers have to think about whether they have enough cigarettes to get them through whatever activity they are engaged in. As more and more places prohibit smoking, smokers must spend a considerable amount of time looking forward to their next cigarette (the minute they can burst out of the meeting, get out of the cinema, leave the plane, etc.). And, if they are concerned about their behaviour, as most are, they will spend time worrying about its harmful conse-quences (for themselves and others), trying to cut down, and then worrying about failure.

People who are unhappy with different aspects of their bodies and repeatedly want plastic surgery must find ways to save towards their goal. They will also spend much time going over and over their dissatisfactions with their body, deciding which different procedures to have and imagining how everything will be different when the surgery is done.

People who watch excessive TV tend to spend a lot of time thinking about or discussing the characters in their favourite soaps, worrying if they are going to miss an episode or making mental notes to set the video, and relating characters' thoughts and feelings to themselves.

You might find it revelatory to think about your own problem activity and calculate just how much time it takes up, both in your thoughts and in carrying it out. We have included a blank box (below) where you can make a note of what you come up with. You may be surprised to find that it takes up a much bigger chunk of your life than you realised.

■ **How I spend time thinking about my particular problem activity**

2. Do you often overdo it, without realising or intending to?

People who engage in an addictive behaviour of any sort begin to find that, repeatedly, they have taken more of the 'drug' than they intended. We use the word 'drug' here to stand for any addictive activity, because that activity is exactly like a drug for you. You indulge in it because you want a quick high. But it starts to get out of hand.

So, perhaps you intend to have just one or two glasses of wine to relax, and end up drinking the whole bottle. You call in at the pub for a 'swift half' and stay till closing time. You snort 'just one' line of coke and keep going back for more. You light a cigarette and find you already have one burning in the ashtray. You switch on the television to catch one programme and find yourself still glued to the screen in the early hours of the morning. You promise yourself only one biscuit and end up eating the whole packet. You go into a bookshop to buy a particular book

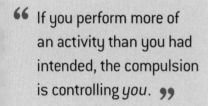

If you perform more of an activity than you had intended, the compulsion is controlling *you*.

but can't resist buying three more that catch your eye – yet you don't get round to reading any of them. You are surfing the internet and decide to bet cash online in a game of poker but soon find yourself playing for hours. Or perhaps you spend more and more time visiting internet chatrooms, not as a 'treat' but as a regular means of blocking out problems, rows with partners or children, or avoiding responsibilities.

Use the blank box below to note down memorable occasions when you have unintentionally gone overboard with your problem activity.

■ **How I have unintentionally 'overdone it'**

If you look at what you have written, you can see that what began as a pleasure is now often or always out of control. You are never in control if you perform more of an activity than you had intended; the compulsion is controlling *you*.

"I can hold my drink"

MANY PEOPLE who drink to excess use the fact that they can drink a lot and not seem drunk as a way of denying to themselves that they have a drink problem. To their way of thinking, if they can keep on drinking and not experience the effects of too much alcohol, or not until long after their drinking partners are under the table, they don't have a problem. But nothing could be further from the truth. This is exactly what is meant by the symptom of tolerance.

Not getting drunk, when drinking heavily, is like not feeling pain when you injure yourself. There is, in fact, an extremely rare condition that causes those born with it to be unable to feel pain of any kind but, far from this being a joyous state of affairs for them, their bodies suffer terribly. They have no way of knowing when they sprain or even break a limb, burn themselves or injure themselves in some other serious way until they see the evidence of the injury or find they can't use the injured part. By that time they may have worsened the damage, like driving on a flat tyre. People who are incapable of feeling pain are unlikely to live beyond their 30s.

Most of us get over-talkative, giddy, unsteady and eventually tend to feel extremely sick, when we have drunk too much alcohol. But, like those who don't experience pain, people who can drink a lot without experiencing the heady or ▶

3. Do you need to engage in the activity more and more, to get any satisfaction?

Think back, if you can, to when you started the activity that is now causing you a problem. Did you engage in it as much as you do now? We are pretty certain that your answer is no, whatever your addiction. At first, engaging in it brought enjoyment, perhaps a rush of pleasure or excitement. Perhaps the activity was illicit, such as underage smoking (in which case the thrill of smoking might have masked or lessened the fact that the first cigarette tasted awful). Or maybe you were taking illegal drugs or illegal risks (such as driving fast without a licence). Perhaps the aim of the activity was to push away physical or mental pain, through the use of alcohol or prescribed medication for instance, or you wanted to comfort yourself, by eating chocolate or cake for instance. Perhaps problems had overwhelmed you and you worried so much you became depressed.

Originally it seemed to do the 'trick' for you: bringing

nauseous effects lack a healthy warning system. Maybe they never had it; maybe the warning gets overridden or, for some, the response weakens over time. Whatever the reason, the effect is the same as for people who can't feel pain – serious damage to the body without realising it.

sudden pleasure or blocking out the pain. But gradually you have had to increase the activity, just to get some degree of satisfaction – but strangely never ever as much as when you first started. You don't smoke one or two cigarettes a day; you more likely smoke 20 or 30 or 40 or more. You don't make occasional forays to special shops to buy costly clothes; you go more and more often and rarely wear what you buy. You don't send the occasional text message; you need to keep on sending and receiving them. All of it is for no more gain than when you did it just once, the first time. If this is you, you have become what is termed 'tolerant' of your particular 'drug'. Little doses don't do the job anymore.

■ **How I've increased engaging in my problem activity**

At the start

After a year

Now

There is a very simple explanation for why we become tolerant of addictive actions, resulting in the need to engage in them more and more and more. Fortunately, this explanation helps point us directly towards a solution, as we shall show later in this section.

In the blank box (on the left opposite), recall, if you can, how often you engaged in your problem activity at the start, after a year and now.

4. Do you get withdrawal symptoms if you restrain yourself?

Withdrawal symptoms, of course, are largely what keep us performing our addictive actions, even after the pleasure rush has gone out of them. Everyone knows that heroin users may go through a hellish physical experience when trying to go 'cold turkey'. Many people claim that the withdrawal symptoms associated with stopping smoking cigarettes are as bad or even worse. Drinkers may get the shakes. People who overeat may experience the unpleasant pangs of what they consider hunger. But even people whose activities are not concerned with taking some substance into their bodies commonly experience withdrawal symptoms, such as agitation, discomfort, inability to concentrate, restlessness, depressed mood or a physical sensation associated with perceived loss. In severe cases, withdrawal symptoms can even lead to acute psychosis and sometimes death by suicide.

So when we continue with an addictive behaviour we are seeking relief from such symptoms – not so much the huge high (that is largely gone), but a halt to the uncomfortable withdrawal effects. In fact, we may end up needing to engage in the compulsive activity purely to allow us to function relatively 'normally' – in other words, we need the problem activity simply to enable us to live life as others, who have no need of such unhealthy props, live it. (And eventually even that stops being possible, as we will show later.)

The withdrawal effects are always the opposite of whatever the 'drug' delivered. If drinking makes you feel relaxed and confident, withdrawal will make you feel tense and 'wired up'. If cocaine makes you feel high, withdrawal will generate a deep, depressed feeling. If having compulsive sex, gambling or eating a prohibited food lifts your mood briefly, not doing it brings you down.

> 66 The good news is that withdrawal need not be like this at all. 99

Although experiencing these kinds of symptoms is one of the indicators of addiction, the good news is that withdrawal need not be like this at all. (We will explain the physiological reasons for this later in this section.)

5. Have you stopped your initial activity but substituted another addictive behaviour for it?

This is a very insidious one. We may think we have got control over our smoking, eating, TV watching, etc., but now we've got another problem instead. So while we may have put a halt to one particular activity, we haven't gained control of addictive behaviour itself. For instance, very commonly, people who stop smoking start to eat or drink more, or continually chew gum. One woman one of us helped started exercising frantically, purely as a means of keeping busy instead of smoking. People who seek help for stopping smoking often find that their real addiction was actually to overeating – they took up smoking as a means of keeping the addictive eating and weight gain under control. People whose addiction involves an activity, rather than ingesting or imbibing, often, on quitting, throw themselves into work or excessive sport to compensate. And so on.

> 66 Switching one activity for another means we haven't gained control of addictive behaviour itself. 99

Make a note in the blank box overleaf if you have ever switched addictive behaviours in an attempt to beat a primary addiction.

■ **Examples of how I've switched addictive behaviours**

■ **Times when I have tried to stop/cut down my problem behaviour**

6. Have you made at least a few attempts to quit?

When people are dependent on a substance or activity, they often make repeated efforts to stop or cut down – repeated because they fail. The fact that you have read this far means you probably want to stop your problem activity and therefore may already have made persistent or unsuccessful attempts to quit. Perhaps the attempts were half hearted, because it is hard to stay strong when withdrawal effects kick in. Perhaps, as a means of lessening the feelings of guilt and disappointment at failing yet again, you told yourself that you could stop if you *really* put your mind to it. (But, secretly, you worry about whether that's true.) Perhaps, as is common, you managed to stop for quite lengthy periods and then, suddenly, you succumbed to the addiction again – perhaps baffled as to why.

Although repeated, failed attempts to quit are a sign of addiction (i.e. it is too difficult to stop, for whatever reason), this is a good sign, all the same. There is always a healthy part of you that knows the addiction is wrong and that you are cheated by it. Sometimes that knowledge is outwardly denied ("My grandfather smoked 40 cigarettes a day and lived till he was 90"; "I do it because I like it and that is more important to me than living forever"; "It's my life and I'll do what I want with it"). But somewhere inside you there is a nagging concern and discomfort that makes you want to change things.

Until picking up this book, you just hadn't yet found the way to stop and stay stopped.

In the blank box on page 18, note down any times you can recall when you made efforts to quit or significantly cut down on your problem activity, and for how long you were successful.

7. Does engaging in the activity badly affect other areas of your life?

Addictions can have a severe and sometimes devastating impact on other aspects of life, such as your health, job performance, social life, family responsibilities and relationships. If you give this some thought, you may realise that the effects are more far reaching than you have realised.

Clearly, for instance, addictive behaviours such as smoking, drinking, binge eating, drug taking and risk taking are highly likely to have a negative impact on your health. But other addictive behaviours such as gambling, excessive computer-game playing or television watching can also have physical effects, if they lead to your having less sleep than your body needs. And, while exercise is healthy, over exercise can reduce the power of your immune system (athletes tend to suffer more respiratory infections than those who take a normal amount of exercise).

In addition, the stress associated with addictive activities takes its toll, mentally and physically. If you are constantly worrying about when you can get your next 'fix', plotting ways to deceive others into thinking you are engaged in something else, working out how to afford it, fit it in, feeling guilty, being anxious, etc., the strain on your system is enormous! So no one who engages in addictive behaviours is likely to experience tip-top health. And it is another sure sign of addiction if people persist in an addictive activity when it has already seriously affected their health – as in the case of those who continue to smoke even after a heart attack or after having had limbs amputated, due to severe damage caused to blood circulation, and those who continue to drink, even after suffering liver and brain damage.

But the effects are more widespread than the impact on your health. If you are spending more and more time on your problem activity, you may well find that you are spending less and less time with your family or partner or real friends. Look back at the first box you filled in, about time spent on your problem behaviour. All the time that you have identified is taken away from your normal life. You may even have developed the disastrous and utterly mistaken belief that satisfaction and real meaning in life are generated only by your compulsive behaviour, because it is only when you are engaged in it that you feel good or at least OK. As a result, perhaps you are lying to the people who are closest to you, in your need to find ways to carry out your addiction in secret.

When people are really 'hooked', they are likely to give less and less attention to their jobs or other responsibilities, because these things become less important to them. Job performance or duties as a parent may consequently suffer. Similarly, they may withdraw from people they know socially or from recreational activities they have previously enjoyed, eventually becoming more and more isolated. (Or they may associate only with people who share the same addiction.) It isn't just the traditional drug addict whose life unravels in this way. It can happen, albeit to varying degrees, whatever your problem activity.

In the last blank box (below), try to think of all the ways in which your own problem activity has had an unwanted effect on any aspects of your life.

■ **How my problem activity has negatively affected areas of my life**

If you answered YES to at least four of the seven questions we have asked, your behaviour is addictive.

Addiction is widespread for a good reason

This book is for everyone, so we don't particularly want to swamp you with technical statistics, but we will include a few facts and figures here, just to make a highly valuable point. About a third of British adults and a quarter of teenagers smoke. At least six million men and three million women continually exceed the safe limits for alcohol. Half of British 15-year-olds drink alcohol regularly, consuming, on average, about 10 units a week. Deaths from cocaine-related overdoses have reached record levels, with a year-on-year increase of nearly 50 per cent in the numbers of people dying from abuse of the drug since 1998.

One in seven people have tried cannabis, a drug that accounts for up to 80 per cent of illegal drug use. Around 13 million people have tried online poker, with £40m staked across at least 210 sites every day. Between one and two per cent of women in the UK are now estimated to suffer from sex addiction. A fifth of the population is dependent on caffeine. And so it could go on.*

* These statistics are drawn from figures released by the Department of Health, the World Health Organisation and various addiction charities.

Clearly we are drawn in vast numbers to activities with addictive potential. Indeed, it is likely that most people are overly dependent on something or other. It may not be a full-blown addiction but plenty of people don't feel ready to get going in the mornings until they have had a couple of cups of coffee and many more just *have* to have a biscuit or two with their cup of tea. Plenty of others can't relax properly at a social occasion without several alcoholic drinks and some, men particularly, can only express affection through sex. Some people voraciously read newspapers or books; the very act of reading or scanning for information being as important to them as the content or quality of what is being read – they feel 'lost' without their daily fix of reading material.

> 66 Why do we need to perform more and more of our addictive activity only to get less and less of a buzz from it? 99

For all too many individuals, however, over-engaging in an activity does lead to addiction, with all the accompanying costs to health, relationships, work, finances and social life. And, as we have just been discussing, isn't it strange that, despite these huge costs to ourselves and our loved ones, we actually need to perform more and more of the problem activity, just to get less and less of a buzz from it! Eventually, in most cases, we do it mainly to stop ourselves from feeling utterly terrible rather than to gain pleasure. We are seeking relief, not euphoria.

So, why would nature let such a state of affairs exist? With so many people addicted to something or other, how can our species have survived, let alone flourished? There must surely be more to this than meets the eye. And indeed there is.

We are all so vulnerable to addiction because it arises from behaviour that is totally natural and desirable, indeed crucial to our survival and continuing evolution. But addiction itself is not 'natural'. Addiction is the result of this natural biological system going awry, or being 'hijacked'.

Sounds confusing? Preposterous?
Well it's not, as you will see.

Why addiction is a hijacker

It is unlikely that you will have heard of this explanation for addiction before. It was formulated by Joe Griffin, one of the authors of this book, who, in his psychotherapeutic work, spent many years specialising in treating a wide range of addictions. He kicked his own smoking habit decades ago but he was still, until recently, puzzled by his own propensity to drink too much at family get-togethers and celebrations. As a result he found himself pondering the following questions.

■ Why would our biological mechanisms have evolved such seemingly bizarre, often harmful behaviours as the ones we have described above?

■ Why would we develop the capacity to keep switching off the pleasure we derive from undesirable activities (such as drinking, gambling, shopping, caffeine or whatever), so that we have to indulge in them even more, to get a similar but reduced effect?

■ And why should it be in our natures to feel awful if we *stop* drinking the poisons in alcohol or smoking the toxins in cigarettes or performing compulsive activities – so much so that we feel compelled to continue our destructive course, just to avoid the pain or discomfort of withdrawal symptoms?

It seemed to him as if nature had screwed up in a big way and actually designed us to become addicts of one kind or another!

We know, from numerous evolutionary studies since the time of Charles Darwin, that when creatures have particular characteristics that don't aid survival they tend not to reproduce very well, and therefore die out – what is commonly known as 'the survival of the fittest'. Most characteristics that persist in a living organism are there to aid survival, be it thick fur on animals that live in cold regions, a particular shape of bird's beak, suited to the gathering of particular foods, or any number of the complex behaviours developed by humans. So why have we developed and retained the ability to become addicted when addiction harms us and is completely 'anti-life'?

There must, Joe reflected, be another use for the biological mechanism that drives addiction – one that aids life rather than destroys it. Or, more accurately, the mechanism that gives us the unwelcome side effects produced by addiction must be fundamental to life. What could it be? What possible purpose could be served by a mechanism that turns *down* the pleasure dial when we repeatedly perform any behaviour that initially

> 66 There must be another, beneficial, use for the biological mechanism that drives addiction ... 99

gave us pleasure? Eventually he came up with an explanation that not only makes enormous sense but also accounts for every paradoxical aspect of addiction *and* shows us how best to beat it. It is this.

The carrot ...

As human beings, we have many needs – for instance, for warmth, shelter, security, food and drink, attention, connection to others, intimacy, autonomy and to be stretched, which gives us a sense that our lives are meaningful. (We call these needs human 'givens' because they are programmed into us from our genes.) Every living creature has innate needs and instinctively attempts to get its needs met in the environment. And this instinctive drive is aided by the experience of satisfaction or pleasure. Eating, drinking, having sex, learning something new – all these are fundamental activities, crucial to our survival, for which nature rewards us with pleasurable sensations. Thus countless species, most particularly ours, have evolved into the more complex creatures they are today because they had the curiosity to try out something new and found that satisfying.

For instance, long ago something once led someone to pick up a stone and, for the first time, fashion it into a tool, and, because the results were satisfying – survival was made easier – others started to follow suit. But the rush of pleasure experienced, when first doing this, would have dropped, once rudimentary tool-making became run of the mill. It would,

however, have risen again when people realised how to make *different* tools or to use the same tool for different purposes. In our own time, it is the satisfaction that comes from discovery and mastery

> 66 Nature rewards us with pleasurable sensations when we meet our innate needs ... 99

that gives rise to technological developments, creative skills, knowledge about the universe, and so forth.

The 'pleasure dial', Joe realised, is nature's ingenious means of encouraging us to keep our behaviour creative and flexible, so that we can continually adapt to an ever-changing environment. We need to try new things to further the development that in turn aids our survival and, to encourage us to do this, we need to be rewarded with pleasure (the carrot). But, if we kept experiencing the same high amount of pleasure each time we repeated an action, there would be no impetus for us to develop further. We would be a species of automatons, compulsively repeating the same limited enjoyable behaviours. So, in order for us to evolve further and to develop new behaviours to get our innate needs met more and more effectively, we needed to be proactive. Without the pleasure dial to stimulate action, we wouldn't have survived as a species, or climbed the evolutionary ladder, because we would have had no capacity or inclination to adapt and respond to changing circumstances and environmental challenges. As a result, we wouldn't even have advanced as far as the Stone Age.

Instead, then, although we can still experience a certain amount of pleasure or satisfaction when carrying out a routine task, that rush of pleasure, that 'high' we seek, comes only when we experience something new. In this way our own biological systems impel us to keep looking for novel ways to get our needs met and to stretch and challenge ourselves.

... and the stick

So how does nature ensure that, once we have learned a new useful skill or activity, or appreciated a more refined perception, we don't drop it in our never-ending search for new 'highs'? Certainly, turning down the pleasure dial wouldn't be sufficient in itself to keep us on track – we might still easily abandon altogether some of the activities that no longer give us such a buzz. And so this is where the role of withdrawal (the 'stick') comes in. We are encouraged to continue with routine, less dramatically pleasurable but still necessary, activities because we experience discomfort if we don't.

The 'couch potato'

Let's give an example. John spends far too much time slouching in front of the television, eating beer and crisps, and this is starting to have bad effects on his health. His doctor has advised him to take regular exercise, so John starts walking a mile a day. When he set off, he feels as if he has a mountain to climb. But he soon realises that he feels a lot more energetic and lively when he has finished his walk. As his doctor recommended, he gradually increases his walks to three miles a day, all the time feeling better and better.

But, after a few months of walking three miles a day, he ceases to get the same buzz out of it. He is bored with the walking, so he thinks he'll give it a miss for a while. However, as soon as he slumps in front of the TV again, he gets a nagging feeling that something is wrong. He is slightly uncomfortable, mentally and physically. Those are the withdrawal symptoms. They are nature's way of urging John to carry on but, simultaneously, to look for ways to put new interest into his activity. Perhaps he might decide to walk with a friend, vary his route, increase the length of his walk one day and reduce it the next, or perhaps he might decide to take up a different kind of exercise – a challenging sporting activity.

We are not saying that we need to vary every single activity we master. If we like tea, we don't have to try different varieties in order to keep enjoying the taste, or to learn the Karma

Sutra, to keep on enjoying sex. But, as a species, we do thrive on a certain amount of variety. Not many people would like to eat exactly the same food at every meal or to experience no novelty of any kind during their day, whether a new challenge or just an interesting conversation. Indeed, the fashion and entertainment industries thrive on feeding our insatiable demand for novelty. But we all derive our *greatest* highs from doing or achieving something new. (That's why Olympic gold medalists, seemingly at the pinnacle of their achievement, still seek to challenge themselves further – for instance, to win *three* golds, or beat their own world records. And it is also why businessmen don't just stop once they've made their first fortune; they continue to start up new businesses.)

Why being addicted is just chasing 'fool's gold'

So addiction derives from something very natural – the desire for the high that nature gives us when we master something new. Indeed, the more passionate and curious people are about life, the greater their vulnerability to addiction, because they are always open to something new and are keen to experience as much as possible, as strongly as they can. But, alas, addiction is the cheating high, the quick fix, the blind alley that leads nowhere, and all that passion and curiosity is wasted. It is a perversion of the natural learning system in our brains. Whereas nature's carrot and stick keep us focusing outwards, addiction sucks us in. It doesn't want to let go until it has bled us dry, destroyed our psychological and physical health and collapsed our confidence and self-esteem. Furthermore it often won't be satisfied with destroying just us but will seek to destroy our most important relationships as well. (We will explain exactly how all this

> 66 Natural highs are the real thing, the *truly* satisfying experiences. 99

happens, when we look at expectation and craving.)

There is a pale, brass-yellow mineral, called iron pyrites, which amateur prospectors often naively mistake for gold, hence its nickname, 'fool's gold'. But fool's gold would not exist if there were not such a substance as real gold. And so it is with addiction. The highs an addict experiences mimic the natural highs, just as fool's gold masquerades as real gold, but there *are* natural highs to be had, just as there is real gold to be found. Natural highs are the real thing, the *truly* satisfying experiences.

It's important to take this idea in as it represents your route map out of addiction.

The natural 'high'

Although, as we've said, countless numbers of people compulsively perform certain activities, *the majority of people do not.*

Why is it, as we are so vulnerable to becoming addicted, that most people have not got full-blown addictions to contend with? It is because most of us get sufficient important needs met in the way we live our lives that we do not succumb to the fool's gold of addiction.

As we have said, we all have basic emotional needs. These include the needs for security, attention, volition and control, status, emotional connection to other people and to be stretched in what we do, which makes life meaningful. When our needs are met, we feel fulfilled in different areas of our lives. If our lives are peopled with those we love and who love us, are filled with activities we enjoy and that challenge or engross us, offer new experiences and opportunities, and have their share of responsibilities and duties we deem important to fulfil, we will not succumb to addiction. (Smoking, however, is a slightly different matter – see the box on page 37.)

Addictions stop us from getting our needs met in healthy balance. Unconsciously, we know this. And we choose not to do something pleasant to excess if it will get in the way of something that, emotionally, we value more. In other words, something with a stronger emotional pull will be more powerful for us than the allure of a transient pleasant activity. For instance, people don't tend to stay up till the early hours of the morning watching TV, playing computer games or drinking with friends if they have an important occasion to

Eating disorders are addictions too

ALTHOUGH NOT often thought of in this way, what is termed an 'eating disorder' is actually a compulsive, addictive behaviour. The fact that some people are willing to risk their health, often their very life, in pursuit of this behaviour, makes that clear.

In addition, anorexia and bulimia are both means of seeking the emotional intensity, 'the high', that all addicts are chasing. For instance, it is well known that starvation can create intense feelings of satisfaction, derived from feeling power and control over oneself or others, and feelings of purity and goodness. Starvation may also stimulate the production of endorphins, the feel-good chemicals released by the body in response to pain. Endorphins are natural opiates and may reinforce addictive behaviours.

People with bulimia may seemingly wish to achieve the perfect body, but what keeps them addicted is actually the excitement or change of mood associated with 'acting out' the process. Thinking about bingeing, planning it, buying the food, eating the food – all produce an increasing intensification of emotional experience. Indeed, sufferers from bulimia commonly say that they don't even taste most of the food they binge on. Similarly, anorexics are more interested in the process of getting thinner rather than aiming for a particular desired body size.

attend the following day. Instead, they choose to put a limit on their pleasure, so that they can give their best the next day, because what will be happening – be it giving a presentation, attending a daughter's wedding or taking a driving test – has more meaning for them.

> **" Addictions stop us getting our needs met in healthy balance. "**

Sometimes, of course, we may know intellectually that we should call a halt but we go on with an activity because we are so in the moment, and gripped by the excitement of it. The result is we suffer the next day. And, if as a result of doing that too often, our job or our marriage is on the line, we quickly have to weigh up and act on what is more important for us, emotionally. If we reach the point where we don't choose the job or the relationship or whatever, something must be missing in our lives, which we are trying to replace with the cheap high of addiction.

All addiction results from needs not being met

We are protected from addiction when our lives are fulfilling. All addiction results from important needs not being met.

This may come as a shock to you, or it may not. Maybe you are well aware of what is missing in your life – you drink because you are lonely; you eat because you are bored. But, very often, people don't realise that they are seeking the quick high of addiction to fill some other hole in their life. They may

"Smoking isn't any different"

TYPICALLY PEOPLE begin smoking in their teens, a time of experimentation when young people feel uncertain about their role and place in the community. If their peers smoke, they are very likely to take it up too, to satisfy that need for acceptance and status within the group. It then quickly becomes a serious habit.

Smoking is a more insidious addiction than most others because it became legitimised in society (although that is being strongly questioned now). It has been acceptable to smoke while carrying out normal activities, such as working, sitting in restaurants, making phone calls, enjoying social occasions, etc. Smoking doesn't cloud judgement, as alcohol and illicit or overused prescribed drugs do. It doesn't usually lead to the loss of one's job or relationships.

But if starting to smoke appeared to satisfy some needs, continuing to smoke actually stops needs being met. It can be a means of avoiding being fully engaged in situations (non-smokers concentrate better than smokers, despite smokers imagining that cigarettes help them focus) or of creating distance between people – a distracting displacement activity. Increasingly, too, in today's climate of growing non-acceptance of smoking, smokers may avoid going to social events in places where they cannot smoke. They may avoid taking up jobs in non-smoking companies. Also, if they are in a non-smoking environment, they may spend much time wishing they could get away for a smoke, instead of fully enjoying the moment.

think they 'have it all'. Or they may think they are quite happy, smoking joint after joint of cannabis every night, to wind down after work or when the baby is in bed, perhaps not questioning whether, perhaps, they are using it to dull the realisation that they hate their job or that they are no longer free to take off at any time and travel the world. Or perhaps they don't recognise what is missing because they have filled their life with their addiction and surrounded themselves with others who share their addiction, as drinkers, drug addicts and gamblers commonly do.

> 66 Addiction is the learning mechanism of the brain switched to *de*struct, instead of *con*struct. 99

But no one who engages in a compulsive activity can be getting all their needs met in a healthy way. (If you were getting all your needs met, there wouldn't be the space to fit in the addiction.) The two things are mutually exclusive. Addiction is the other side of the coin, the learning mechanism of the brain switched to *de*struct, instead of *con*struct. It undermines whatever needs are or were being fulfilled in a healthy way and further prevents you from finding real satisfactions.

The sense of something missing in their lives is what leads many people to swap one addiction for another equally addictive activity, even an apparently healthy one. So the ex-smoker or gambler or drug addict starts to exercise compulsively or eat more compulsively or spend hours doing another activity, such as yoga. The need the original addiction was masking is still not being met, so they take on a new one.

Very commonly, people turn or return to addictive behaviours when they experience a major loss in their lives, such as bereavement, redundancy or disability, and important needs cease to be met. Addiction often goes hand in hand with depression, which also occurs when needs aren't met and when people unwittingly catastrophise what is happening in their lives.*

You've got to get a life!

The long-term answer to addiction, then, is to create for yourself a lifestyle in which your needs are healthily and satisfyingly met. This is the way that you can learn the discipline to conquer and contain any addictive tendencies you may have. And the best thing is that it can actually be a pleasurable way to go about beating addiction! By our method, you increase pleasure rather than enduring suffering. There really is no need for a lot of pain and discomfort when stopping an addictive habit.

---

* For specific help with depression, see our book *How to lift depression ... fast*.

How do we know that 'having a life' eliminates addiction?

There is much evidence that being happy and fulfilled eliminates the need for addictive activity. Here are a few powerful examples.

Evidence from 'Rat Park'

In a famous experiment known as Rat Park, rats that were kept singly in small cages eagerly drank morphine-laced water sweetened with sugar, which they were able to access by pressing a lever, rather than drink the water that was also available. By contrast, rats kept in pairs in larger pens consumed far less of the morphine concoction. And rats kept in groups in a very large enclosure, which was as similar as possible to the kind of habitat that rats love best (Rat Park), consistently chose water over the morphine mixture. They would happily drink water sweetened with sugar, if it was offered, but not if morphine was added. When the rats were switched between the different environments, those that had been the highest 'users' when alone in small cages became the lowest users when living in Rat Park, and vice versa.

Even when all the rats were forced to drink the morphine mixture for two months, only the rats isolated in small cages continued to choose the morphine water when later offered both that and plain water. Those in Rat Park quickly tailed off their morphine consumption.

What the experiment clearly showed was that drug usage depended not on individual biology or character but on whether or how well needs were met. Rats that were confined alone or in cramped conditions, in boring environments that offered nothing to stimulate them, developed the highest reliance on morphine. But even these rats voluntarily reduced their consumption if they were given food treats. They also took less if experimenters made it more difficult to operate the levers that delivered the drug or made the drug available only at unpredictable times.*

Evidence from veteran soldiers

The same effect was powerfully demonstrated in humans. Of the American soldiers who served in Vietnam in the 1970s, 50 per cent were found by researchers to be using heroin. The authorities were highly anxious about what would happen when this large drug-using population returned home at the end of the war (in 1975), so they closely monitored them. To everyone's surprise, only 12 per cent of the veterans continued to use heroin, once they were back with their families and taking up their old lives again.†

* Alexander, B.K., Coambs, R.B. and Hadaway, P.F. (1978). The effects of housing and gender on morphine self administration in rats. *Psychopharmacology*, 58, 175–179.

† Robins, L.N., Helzer, J.E., Hesselbrock, M. and Wish, E. (1980). Vietnam veterans three years after Vietnam: how our study changed our view of heroin. In L. Brill & C. Winick (eds) *The Yearbook of Substance Use and Abuse*. Human Sciences Press.

Eighty per cent gave up use within a year, half of their own accord and half through clinics. Those who didn't manage to give up were those who either had post-traumatic stress disorder or who had broken families, and therefore no one to return to.

Evidence from statistics

There is a massive natural recovery from addiction. For instance, 18–34-year-olds are the heaviest users of alcohol. Consumption drops dramatically in the 35–54 age group. A full half of recovery from addiction is spontaneous – that is, achieved by individuals of their own volition, without any aid from professional sources. Drug use peaks between the ages of 14 and 25 and sometime during that period most users will have stopped, again without professional assistance.

It is no surprise that young people have a high tendency to engage in addictive activities. It is during adolescence and young adulthood that we make the difficult transition from having our needs provided for by others to having to take responsibility for our own wellbeing. It is a turbulent time of maximum insecurity. Drug use changes and largely stops as young people establish themselves further up career ladders, form lasting relationships and start families.* Those who persist with drug use tend to be those who have been socially

* Erickson, P.G. and Alexander, B.K. (1989). Cocaine and addictive liability. *Social Pharmacology*, 3, 249–270.

excluded, physically or emotionally abused, lack jobs and family and suffer emotional difficulties.

Myths about addiction

Perhaps, after reading the previous pages, many of the beliefs you currently hold about addiction no longer seem to fit with the facts as we have described them. If so, it is time to dispel some myths.

Myth 1 – Addiction is a biological disease

Addiction is *not* primarily a biological disease, although some people may find it helpful to think of it that way. This common belief is, strangely, applied to some addictions but not others. How many smokers, for example, think of their smoking as being a biological disease? The following are some widespread ideas about addictions. How do they fit with your own ideas and beliefs?

- Addiction is biological, a disease in its own right
- It is in your genes and you can't do anything to change that
- You need medical treatment and/or the permanent support of a recovery group
- You are either addicted to something or you aren't – there is no middle way – and even if you overcome it, you will always be at high risk of relapse, so you will

need to be hyper-vigilant against temptation for the rest of your life

● You will never be able to manage your addiction unless you acknowledge that you have a disease

● If you need help, an expert on addiction or people who have recovered from addictions are the ones who have most to offer you, and can best support you

● Surrendering to a higher power is the only route to recovery.

You'll notice that beliefs like these shift the responsibility for addiction and for recovering from it away from the individual concerned. However, this doesn't fit with the findings about recovery, spontaneous or otherwise, that we have just described.

Addiction and genes

The fact that addiction often runs in families does not prove that it is primarily genetic in origin. For example, certain people may have a genetic tendency to take risks but that doesn't automatically mean that they will develop a gambling addiction. Instead their risk-taking tendency may lead them to become business entrepreneurs.

Families are close, sometimes claustrophobic, places to grow up in. We learn from the behaviour we see around us. Those with alcoholic parents who become alcoholics themselves may have unwittingly absorbed the belief that 'life is a bitch', that you can't get on top of it and that the way to deal with difficulties is to drown them in drink. Youngsters who grow up in smoking households may, despite all the publicity to the contrary, still assume that there is nothing wrong with the habit if their own parents indulge in it. And children brought up in

> 66 We learn from the behaviour we see around us ... 99

families where smoking cannabis is regarded as normal behaviour may actually be encouraged to smoke it at a young age. For example, Ivan recently worked with a 25-year-old woman who had been introduced to cannabis at the age of seven by her father. When she reached her 13th birthday, he 'treated' her to a snort of cocaine as a birthday present!

Equally, there are very many people who are completely against alcohol because of the miseries they experienced growing up with an alcoholic parent. And there are countless young people who reject the idea of smoking because they have seen the bad effects on the health of their parents or grandparents and have taken in the health messages received at school.

In other words, different people exposed to the same kind of experiences take away different messages from them. Even if genes predispose certain individuals to take away one message rather than another, that still doesn't stop them from choosing a different path, if they are shown how to do so.

Now look at this very different list of beliefs which for many people is far more empowering.*

- Your particular addiction is your way of coping with yourself and your world, as it is at present. It stems from problems or difficulties you have, or disappointments you have experienced.

- The way to beat it is to identify why you 'need' addiction at the moment (which emotional needs aren't being met in your life) and make changes, such as developing practical and social skills, doing different things and spending time with different people in different places, that will make addiction unnecessary. Identify the solutions that work for you.

- Addiction is not an all-or-nothing state. All behaviour changes, according to circumstances and our emotional responses to those circumstances.

- Far from needing to acknowledge that you have a 'disease', you need to build on and reinforce the positives qualities and talents you have that can lead you quite naturally out of addiction.

- Those who do not have addictions, particularly family

---

* In creating this list, we have built on the work of inspired researcher and innovator in the field of addiction, Stanton Peele, the first to develop a 'social learning model' of addiction, in contrast to the 'disease model'. See Peele, S. (1995). *Diseasing of America*. Lexington Books.

members, friends and colleagues who are living healthy, productive lives, are the people it is most helpful to spend your time with.

● Developing your self-awareness and your own innate power are what will most help you to overcome addiction. Getting better is about understanding what is *really* going on, not about beliefs.

It is also a myth that addiction is always a progressive disorder and all that can be done to keep it at bay is to have lifelong support. Of course we are not denying that very many people are grateful to and rely on support groups but these can, however, become a problem for some people who, through constant talking about their addiction (alcoholics, overeaters, self-harmers, etc.), continue to identify with it instead of outgrowing it. (Nicotine is generally acknowledged to be highly addictive. But how many of the 50 million or more smokers worldwide who have successfully stopped smoking feel the need to be in a life-long support group?) Sometimes people can even become addicted to their support group – especially if it meets a need for them, such as for attention or social contact. Joe once worked with a woman whose husband, a recovered alcoholic, would abandon his family responsibilities the moment he received a call from a recovering alcoholic needing support. On one occasion, he even left his wife and children during Christmas lunch and didn't return all day.

If you decide the 'disease' view of addiction isn't for you, then consign it to the dustbin and take on the 'social change' approach. You will then have a range of powerful options. How you decide to institute change can be based on what best suits you and the life you lead. However, should you decide that the 'disease' model suits your needs, the information and many of the techniques given in this book will still be very helpful to you.

Myth 2 – Withdrawal is agony

If, like many people, you have ever tried to give up your compulsive activity, you will know for yourself what form withdrawal symptoms might take. Agitation, restlessness, inability to concentrate, unpleasant physical sensations, the feeling that life is not worth living any more – with symptoms like these, how can we say that such an experience isn't agony? How can the experience of withdrawal not be an overwhelmingly powerful one if it can drive a person out of the house at midnight in freezing, torrential rain, in search of a garage or an all-night shop that sells cigarettes or chocolate or whisky? How can it not be powerful if sometimes it can even drive people to kill themselves?

But we are not saying that such experiences aren't powerful or can't be overwhelming. Rather, what we are saying is that withdrawal *doesn't have to be like that*. Perhaps the best way to illustrate this is with a little story.

The murderous smoker

A woman called Mary once came to see Joe for help with stopping smoking. The next day she rang the receptionist at the clinic where he worked, begging to speak to him. "I'm so desperate for a cigarette that I'm ready to murder my children," she shouted, clearly in a terrible panic. The receptionist was so alarmed by this that she urged her to ring back in 20 minutes when, she promised, Joe would be free and could speak to her.

Mary rang back on the dot, 20 minutes later. Joe knew that, in her highly aroused, emotional state, she would be unable to see reason. She was in the grip of black-and-white thinking, which stops us seeing that there are many ways to respond to difficult situations. It is the thinking style of what is known as the emotional brain, a primitive part of the brain originally concerned just with danger. Should we fight or should we flee? Should we eat it or would it make us sick? When there is danger, we need to act fast, not deliberate over all the possibilities. But when we get overly emotionally aroused and we aren't in danger, that thinking style stops us from seeing the wider picture. We need to get some perspective back.

> ❝ Emotional arousal stops us seeing the wider picture ... ❞

So Joe's first action was to help Mary to calm her breathing (using the 7/11 technique that we describe in the second part of this book). Once she had calmed down enough to listen and take in what he was saying, Joe told her, "I'm going to ask you a very important question and I want you to think carefully before you answer. Have you ever had a desperately painful toothache?"

"Of course!" Mary replied, at once.

"Can you remember a specific time?"

"Oh, I most certainly can!"

"Tell me, which was worse? The desperately painful toothache or the desire you feel now for a cigarette?"

"The toothache was worse," Mary said, without hesitation.

"Have you ever had a mild, nagging, persistent toothache, Mary?"

"Yes, I have."

"Can you think back to an actual time?"

Mary thought for a moment. "Yes, I can."

"Which is worse?" asked Joe. "That nagging toothache that won't go away or the desire for a cigarette?"

Silence. "If I'm honest, the toothache."

"OK. When you get a desire for a cigarette, how long does it last?"

Mary recovered a bit of her vehemence at this point. "I'd say a good five minutes!"

"So, let's get this clear," said Joe. "You are ready to murder your children for a degree of discomfort that is milder than a slight, nagging toothache and which lasts for just five minutes?"

Mary burst out laughing. Now, in a much calmer state, she was no longer blowing her physical experience out of all proportion, through her over-emotional reaction to it. Instead she could stand back and see how ridiculous her position was. This was enough to enable her to get her really rather mild withdrawal symptoms into perspective, and to continue coping with them and staying off cigarettes.

Withdrawal symptoms *have* to be mild

If you think back to nature's carrot and stick mechanism, you'll see that withdrawal symptoms *have* to be mild. When nature turns down the pleasure dial, when the couch potato no longer finds going for a regular walk so satisfying, and stops it for a while, it is a mild, nagging feeling of discomfort that is experienced, not an enormous pain! Even if we feel hungry – one of our most basic of appetites, because we can die without food – we know we can happily override a hunger pang without a second thought when we have something interesting or important to do instead of eating at that moment. If nature made withdrawal symptoms agony, we would be incapacitated – either doubled over in pain or unable to take our minds off the experience and carry on our normal routines. That would compromise our safety – and work against our survival as a species – instead of enhancing it. Yet, as you may have experienced yourself, that terrible pain or inability to get on with ordinary life is indeed what very many people suffer on quitting an addictive activity they have come to rely on. Why? Because they are actually misusing their imaginations to create their intense suffering, just as Mary did.

It is important to realise, however, that we are talking here about the *craving* for a drug, not about the medical symptoms that can be triggered in people who have built up high tolerance levels for a drug and who suddenly stop taking it. In the case of sudden alcohol withdrawal by heavy drinkers, for example, these symptoms can include convulsions and delirium tremens – psychotic symptoms more commonly known as the DTs. These cases need to be medically supervised.

Myth 3 – I'll never manage to stop because I've failed every time before

Contrary to popular belief, the more times you try to stop, the more likely you are to stop your problem activity eventually. Giving up an addiction is part of a process.

Nobody wakes up one morning and just stops being addicted – there is a huge psychological component to addiction. Emotionally, over time, you will have identified more and more with your addictive habit and progressively built a lifestyle around it. That doesn't just evaporate in a second. Just as it takes time for the addictive activity to take up a progressively greater proportion of your life, so it takes time for change to be put into place.

> ** Contrary to popular belief – the more times you try to stop the more likely you are to succeed ... **

The wheel of change

Two psychologists, James Prochaska and Carlo DiClemente, made a study of the way that addicted people come to quit addictions. As a result, they identified what they termed 'the wheel of change', to explain the process people go through when they want to kick a destructive addictive habit.*

Pre-contemplation

The researchers found that initially people are reluctant to admit that a problem may be developing. This is when you are 'in love' with your addiction. You love the jollity of getting drunk with your friends, or the high of taking drugs at a party, or the rush that gambling gives you. Even when faced with the concerns of others, you always have a ready answer that stops you experiencing concern yourself. ("My grand-father smoked 30 cigarettes a day and lived to get a telegram

---

* DiClemente, C.C. and Prochaska, J.O. (1985). Processes and stages of self-change. In S. Shiffman and T.A. Wills (eds). *Coping and Substance Use.* Academic Press.

from the Queen." "I can drink six pints and still drive home." "So what's wrong with being fat? Fat is beautiful.") Prochaska and DiClemente called this the 'pre-contemplation stage' because, at this stage, you give no thought at all to the harm that the addictive activity is doing to your life.

Contemplation

But, gradually, you find you have to perform your addictive activity more and more to achieve less and less effect, and the withdrawal symptoms seem more pronounced when you try to hold back. Doubts about what you are doing may start to creep in. Perhaps you are beginning to be aware that your health is not so good, that your relationships or work are suffering, that you are spending excessively to fund the habit or that the addictive activity is causing you more misery than joy, although you still feel impelled to do it. You feel ambivalent – you want to stop and you don't want to stop. Perhaps you try to cut back and it works for a while. But, very soon, you are back up to the level of addictive activity you were at before. You start saying to yourself, "I don't like this." But, although you are contemplating change, you are still reluctant to make the break.

Determination

At this point, it is as if you are a pair of scales, with the balance tipping one way and then the other. Then something happens that tips the balance decisively in favour of stopping.

Maybe you get some bad news from the doctor. Maybe you hear of something bad that has happened to someone else in your situation. Maybe your awareness of what addiction is doing to you just builds up and up until it reaches the point where you say, "I don't like the price I'm paying for this. It is just not worth it." This stage is like a door opening. If you go through it, you will move on to the next stage. If not, you will turn back to the previous one.

Action

You go through the door. You decide on a strategy for change (working out ways to keep yourself away from your problem activity, which might include seeking treatment), set a time to begin and either stop or drastically cut down.

Maintenance

Now you have to stay stopped. But the truth is, on the first attempt, three out of four people don't manage it. They relapse, and often the result is that they go right round the wheel to the pre-contemplation stage again. It is simply too hard to summon up all that motivation and self-belief to get going again, when, in your own terms, you have failed. It feels more manageable for a time to put out of your mind all thought of the damage addiction does, so relieved are you not to be struggling to stop any more. But very soon, of course, the doubts creep back in, and again you want to find a way to stop.

The good news is this. Although a quarter of people may succeed the first time, in general, the more times you go round on the wheel of change, the more likely you are to get off it. This is because the more times you try and you hit an obstacle, the more you are learning about what works and what doesn't work when handling your addictive activity. All the time, unconsciously, you are adding to the package of skills that, sooner or later, will enable you to kick your habit. So, don't dismiss all the learning you have done by calling it failure! Past attempts can be stepping stones to ultimate success, if we use the lessons that can be learnt from them.

Myth 4 – If I decide to stop, then I'll just stop

People who stop suddenly and successfully are those who have been through the wheel of change and reach the point where they *really* feel that their addiction is doing them more harm than good, and change their lives so that their needs are met in truly satisfying ways. It is never purely a matter of thinking or deciding, because addiction isn't logical. It *can't* be logical. How can it be logical for people to rush out of the house into wind and rain at a time of night when everyone else is cosily tucked up asleep, just to get new supplies of the addictive substance they have run out of? How can it be logical to undergo the amputation of limbs or a quadruple heart bypass or a liver transplant or disabling debt or a broken relationship or a ruined social life, all to keep performing the compulsive activity that often brings no pleasure at all?

Addiction is clever. It knows all your weaknesses, all your failings, and will ruthlessly use them. It has access to all your brain circuits and to your IQ. It has the same IQ as you do! If you are an intelligent person, you will have an intelligent addiction, so don't imagine it is easier to give up if you are smart. Indeed, intelligent people often find it hardest to give up addictions. They say, "I know all this" or "I understand all that but it doesn't make any difference." They don't realise that, if they have a PhD, their addiction has a PhD too! It is *underestimating* addiction that keeps intelligent people trapped in their compulsive activity. You cannot out-think addiction. But there are other ways that you can successfully beat it.

Myth 5 – You need bags of will power

People think of *will power* as if it is a weapon against *won't power* – something you have to summon up with all your strength to beat evil forces. But will power is not a commodity that exists or a substance with a physical presence, like an organ in the body. It is not something that we are allotted certain amounts of, and that some people have more of than others.

As you've seen from the wheel of change, the motivation to break an addictive habit has to come from within you. It is when people are able to view their addictive behaviour dispassionately and truly recognise the impact it is having on their health, their relationships and the futures they had envisaged for themselves, that they come to the point where the price of the addiction is higher than they want to pay. They lose faith in the false promises of their addiction. They begin to see addiction for what it really is: their mortal enemy, not their friend. They realise that freedom from addiction is what they really want. This is what causes will power to emerge.

> **Will power is *not* something we are allotted certain amounts of ...**

Will power is a consequence of the recognition that addiction cheats you and devastates your life, combined with the realisation that you can overcome it, reclaim your freedom and recapture the joy of living. When you recognise that, you *will* want to use your power.

We are now going to look at what causes cravings. When you've read this, you will understand completely why you do have the power to switch off your addiction.

What happens in the brain when you have a craving

We have explained why addiction occurs and the circumstances (needs not being met) in which it is most able to hijack the brain mechanisms that are designed to reward positive, constructive activity with pleasure. The next important thing to understand is *how* it happens. We need to know what is going on in the brain when we crave our problem substance or activity, so that we know how to stop it happening.

And this is where the *expectation theory of addiction* comes in.* We are confident that, once you've read it, you will not only understand your own struggle with addictive behaviour but also find yourself empowered to deal with it healthily and willingly.

The brain, as we know, is a highly complex organ, with billions of nerve cells. But the structures that are the most important for our understanding of addiction are the ones shown in the diagram on page 61. They are the main actors in the drama of addiction. Let's meet them.

The boss and the boss's secretary

Towards the top left of the diagram, you can see a structure that is called the *dorsolateral prefrontal cortex*. This is our work-

---

* Griffin, J (2004). Great expectations. *Human Givens*, 11 (1), 12–19.

ing memory. It is the part of the brain that coordinates our awareness of what is going on at any given moment. It has a sense of who we are, what we are about and what our priorities are. It is where we plan and make decisions and form our expectations for what is going to happen in our lives. As dorsolateral prefrontal cortex is quite a mouthful, we like to call it 'the boss'.*

Below and a bit further to the right, you can see a structure called the *anterior cingulate* – this, in effect, is 'the boss's secretary'.* As is commonly the case when a boss has an efficient secretary, the secretary keeps the wheels of the operation turning and makes the routine or common-sense decisions without bothering the boss. Only when something is out of the ordinary does she need to talk to the boss about it. This is the brain equivalent of running on 'automatic' – all those things we do without conscious thought, such as driving a car or making a cup of tea. When the boss's secretary is in charge, the boss is out to lunch – in brain terms, when the anterior cingulate is active, the dorsolateral prefrontal cortex is inactive.

Further down and further to the centre lies the *hippocampus* – our personal memory store. This is our conscious memory store, where we keep a record of all our important *personal*

---

* We developed our idea of 'the boss' and 'the boss's secretary' from John Ratey's concept of 'the chief executive officer' and 'the executive secretary', to describe the dorsolateral prefrontal cortex and the anterior cingulate structures in the brain. See Ratey, J (2001). *A User's Guide to the Brain*. Little, Brown and Company.

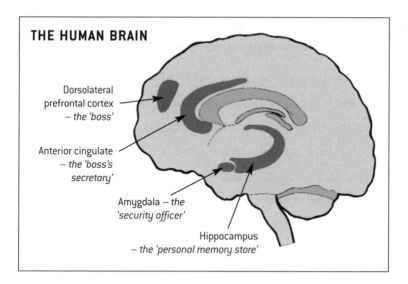

THE HUMAN BRAIN

Dorsolateral prefrontal cortex – *the 'boss'*

Anterior cingulate – *the 'boss's secretary'*

Amygdala – *the 'security officer'*

Hippocampus – *the 'personal memory store'*

experiences. It is the 'storehouse' of all the memories, from the near or distant past, that we can recall at will.

The *amygdala*, just next to it on the left, stores our unconscious emotional memories and conditioned responses, and acts on them. As its most important job is to ensure our survival by alerting us to danger, we'll call it the 'security officer'. Whenever we experience something (hear a sound, sniff a smell, see a movement, etc.), the information is flashed, via means we needn't be concerned with here, to the security officer to be matched to experiences we have had in the past (a process we call pattern matching). He then identifies whether what we are experiencing is alien to us or familiar (and – if familiar – whether it is a security risk) and responds accordingly.

The strange cup of coffee

For instance, the coffee smells 'off'. By pattern matching to previous experiences, the security officer recognises a situation that has been problematic before, so he alerts the boss's secretary. To get her attention, he tags the information with a 'priority mail' sticker – in the form of a brain chemical called *dopamine*. This is essentially a stimulant that works like the drug cocaine and spurs people to want to take action. The more important the security officer thinks the situation might be, the higher the priority he gives it – in real terms, the more dopamine, or emotional charge, is added to make it stand out. We experience this as an emotional charge such as fear, anger, sadness, disgust, joy, etc. In this case, the emotion is disgust.

However, the boss's secretary knows that the security officer can often over-react, as he takes his role extremely seriously. So, on getting the message, she immediately contacts the storehouse, the memory store, to find out what similar situations have occurred in the past. Soon the message comes back that the last time a cup of coffee smelled funny like this we had put gravy granules in the cup by mistake! What we are smelling – and have just been stopped from drinking by the alert security officer – is boiling water with gravy granules, sugar and a dash of milk. On receiving this information, the boss's secretary commends the security officer for his alertness and orders that the 'coffee' be tipped down the sink.

The security officer doesn't always have to enlist the help of the boss's secretary before acting, though. When we are at immediate risk (a tree is about to fall on us, say), the security officer immediately sets off the emergency alarm that signals to the body "All systems go!" and we leg it before the conscious brain has quite registered what is going on. In other words, we act instinctively. The same tends to happen when responses are automatic. We see someone lighting a cigarette or eating a packet of crisps and it triggers the desire (through the pattern-matching process carried out by the security officer) to have a cigarette or packet of crisps ourselves. Very often, we reach for another cigarette or pick up a crisp packet without the boss or boss's secretary even being aware of what we are doing. We are on pure automatic. This is all-important for understanding what's coming next.

The process of withdrawal

Now that we have introduced the lead actors in our drama, we can look at what happens when a craving is experienced – and denied. What we are saying here applies to any addictive activity but we will take smoking as an example.

Jack is a 30-a-day smoker who routinely takes a cigarette out of its pack and lights it up without any conscious thought at all. It is as habitual as rubbing his eyes when he's tired. But just lately he has become concerned about his coughing and has decided that he is not going to smoke any more. He is full of good intentions and today is the day that he has set for quitting.

Normally he has his first cigarette with his cup of coffee at breakfast time. When he lifts his cup of coffee, the security officer makes the pattern match that links coffee with a cigarette and alerts Jack to the fact, via an 'urge to smoke', that he needs to take a cigarette from his pack and light it.

But today is different. The boss has sent down a message, saying that no more cigarettes are to be smoked. So instead of having a cigarette, Jack resists the urge he is feeling. That means that he experiences a withdrawal symptom, instead of, as usually, hardly registering the urge before lighting up another cigarette. At this stage, the withdrawal symptom is very mild. It might be a faint nagging feeling or a slight sensation in the mouth or stomach, a bit like a mild hunger pang.

Thus Jack successfully resists having a cigarette at breakfast. But, by the time he arrives at work, he would normally have had at least three. Now the control monitor situated by the security officer's desk – the hypothalamus, a structure in our brains that monitors the levels of different substances in our blood – shows that Jack's blood nicotine has fallen below its usual level. As nicotine is present in Jack's blood on a daily basis, the control monitor is programmed to act as if it is supposed to be there. It sends out an alert to the security officer to say, "Top up on nicotine!" That, too, triggers a mild withdrawal symptom.

The security officer also assumes that the nicotine is supposed to be there. Perhaps the boss had got it wrong when he said there were to be no more cigarettes? So the security officer decides it is his duty to try to persuade the boss's secretary to change the boss's mind. He sends her a message, marking it as having the highest priority (by adding as much dopamine to the message as is available to him), saying, "PLEASE can we have a cigarette now? We need one!!!"

The boss's secretary receives a lot of post, but anything sprinkled with a lot of dopamine gets precedence; the more dopamine the nearer the top of the pile it goes. Dopamine, as we've said, creates motivation and desire; it spurs us to take action.

Receiving the wrong message

At this stage, as with the peculiar coffee, the boss's secretary doesn't know how to respond to the security officer's alert. She needs to get more information on which to base her decision. So, again, she sends a request to the memory store to find out what smoking cigarettes has done for Jack in the past. She is sent back a file full of memory clips of past experiences connected with smoking. It is at this point that images flash into Jack's mind of how much he has always enjoyed smoking, of how painful it has always been whenever he's tried to deprive himself, and how smoking seems to be connected to all the significant events in his life.

On receiving these clips from the memory store and looking at them, the boss's secretary is alarmed to see that smoking has clearly played an extremely important role in Jack's life. Indeed, from the number of memories recorded, it seems highly essential! "We must have a cigarette!" she shrieks. "I must bring this to the boss's attention immediately." But, in common with most high-powered secretaries, she really likes to run the show herself. So she drafts a letter granting permission to smoke and sends it through to the boss in one of her special attention envelopes – which signify priority over absolutely everything else – with a PostIt note saying, "URGENT! Please sign this straight away!" (In other words, a whole heap more dopamine is added to the chemical message, to make it irresistibly overpowering.) The boss takes one sniff and his desire is overwhelming. All his former resolve is gone. He is out of the frame, and the boss's secretary gets her way. Jack smokes.

> **Whatever your own addictive activity, you can relate it to this scenario.**

Whatever your own addictive activity, you can relate it to this scenario. The desire to shop, to gamble, to have another cup of coffee, to eat a whole loaf of bread, to take another drink, to go to an internet chatroom is awakened. It has become your norm to indulge that desire. You feel niggly, slightly unpleasant sensations of some kind if you don't take steps straightaway or at least make plans to indulge it. But it is only when your brain gets to work and you start fantasising about what pleasures you think your addictive activity gives you – and what pain and discomfort you imagine the denial of it has always caused you – that you get sucked into feeling miserable.

The good news is that this highly unpleasant set of consequences *itself* holds the key to your escape. You are already using the method that will help you beat addiction – using it very forcefully! It is just that you are using it for the wrong purpose, as we shall explain next.

The power of expectation

We are going to introduce you to the most powerful weapon at anyone's disposal in the fight against addiction.

It is expectation.

Expectation is a fundamental thing. Every living being, from the simplest and tiniest to the largest and most complex, comes into the world with a set of expectations about what they will encounter in the world and how they should try to deal with it. These form our instinctive responses – the instinct of a plant to turn towards the sun for light, the rabbit to freeze when it senses danger, the baby to latch on to the nipple for milk, and so on. Expectations, then, concern the needs of living things and the innate resources they can use to help them meet those needs. (A human being's innate needs and resources together make up what we term the human givens.)

Emotions arise from expectations

Of course, the more complex the creature, the more complex its expectations and the greater the variety of ways it develops to meet its needs. Emotions, derived from the Latin *emovere* 'to move outwards, to stir up', are linked to the survival needs and expectations of warm-blooded creatures. Any emotional arousal caused by an expectation – fear of being hurt, desire to have sex, the urge to eat – is discharged when we have taken the appropriate action – moving out of harm's way, making love, enjoying a meal.

Emotions arise from an urge to take some sort of action. They *always* arise from expectations and they follow on from pattern matches made by the amygdala (the security officer). Seeing someone else eating, for instance, can arouse in us a desire to eat; seeing a person we find attractive may arouse sexual desire; being telephoned and invited to a fun party can make us feel happy, even if we were miserable before the phone rang, as we now have an expectation of pleasure. So it is the emotions arising from different expectations that drive us to experience such a varied emotional life – be happy and celebrate, feel desire and seduce, pursue a goal and achieve, be sad and withdraw, be angry and attack, feel disgust and walk away, and so on.

To put this into the context of our imagined 'brain as office' scenario, our emotions are a set of expectations that represent a memo from the security officer to the boss's secretary. The memo says, "This is how I expect you to respond to the information I am supplying you." The security officer has the power to trigger strong emotional arousal, the fight or flight response, but only when it perceives a life-threatening event is happening. It doesn't have the emotional intelligence to instigate any more subtle emotional signals by itself. That has to be done by the boss's secretary.

> 66 If we can stop cravings at the physiological level – all resulting withdrawal symptoms will be mild ... 99

So – if we can stop addictive cravings at the physiological level – (in other words, at the point when the message is sent by the security officer), all resulting withdrawal symptoms will be mild because, as explained earlier, they are designed to be mild for survival reasons. But if we let them reach a psychological level (where the boss's secretary starts adding her own stamp of approval to the message, on the basis of 'positive' information she has received from the memory store), our withdrawal symptoms will become monstrous.

The key word to notice in the last sentence is 'let'. The power is <u>ours</u>. It is the power of expectation that decides the strength of our withdrawal symptoms, and we can choose how we use that power – for or against us.

Why, when we are addicted, does the 'something wonderful' never happen?

As we know, we get less and less pleasure from our addictive activity the more we indulge it. The thrill isn't as great; the effects aren't as reliable. The ninth drink of the night isn't more enjoyable than the first. If we stop to think about it, most cigarettes don't taste good at all. Illicit shopping trips, binges and bouts of gambling, sex or solvent abuse are accompanied by 'downer' doses of guilt. Most of the time we are just trying to stave off the discomfort of withdrawal symptoms. Each time you feel a craving and perform the addictive activity that relieves it, it is no different from deliberately banging yourself on the head with a hammer every four hours, so that you can take an aspirin to relieve you of the resulting headache! You are setting up your own 'headache': the last cigarette, the last go on the slot machine, glass of whisky or computer game played, sets up the withdrawal symptoms that propel you into repeating the cycle.

But now we can see why this is happening. The surge of dopamine into our brains leads us to have high expectations of what is about to happen. It is the motivating chemical. It gets us to do things and, in the normal run of events, that is a good thing. It spurs us to eat and drink, perform tasks, stretch ourselves with new activities and then, when we have achieved what we set out to do, we experience our reward:

satisfaction – mediated by the opiate system in our brains, which supplies our natural equivalent of a heroin high. The dopamine and opiate systems work beautifully in tandem.

However, something very different happens when addiction hijacks these systems. Your expectation then is that something thing really rewarding is going to happen when you take your first drink, cup of coffee, deal the cards, etc. As we know, normally, after a new desire is sated, the pleasure dial is turned down and we go on to

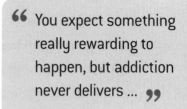

66 You expect something really rewarding to happen, but addiction never delivers ... 99

seek a high from different activities or new variations on old ones. But when needs aren't being met healthily and addictive activity is resorted to, we just repeat and repeat the same activity over and over again. And, although it doesn't deliver the reward or satisfaction that is sought, the amount of dopamine that is generated when we crave an addictive activity or substance, deceives us into *expecting* that we will experience the satisfaction we want, if only we do enough of it. The perpetual illusion is maintained. We don't experience the longed for high level of satisfaction, but we still keep on expecting it.

If your problem activity is drinking, you stimulate the dopamine pathway when you take your first sip. The dopamine tells you something wonderful is going to happen. But it doesn't happen with the first drink. So, convinced it's about to, you have another. And another. Each time you have one, you have the expectation of more pleasure, and so you want to keep drinking. You are conned by the little dopamine rush that you are about to have a more wonderful time, if you just keep on drinking. Perhaps you have a conversation with other drinkers, in which you feel that you are on the brink of some vital new insight that could change the world. You keep drinking and drinking. Then you wake up the next morning with a sore head and realise, perhaps with some embarrassment, what complete claptrap you, and they, were talking.

Indeed, the only thing that switches off the expectation that you will have more pleasure if you have another drink is the toxic effect of *too much* drink. This eventually, by inducing sickness or fatigue, switches off the dopamine flow. Similarly, there comes a point when your system can take no more cigarettes for one day, you feel sick from overeating or exhaustion drives you away from the computer, the gym or the gambling den.

Something wonderful has *not* happened.

Psychologists have tested this out with alcoholics living on the streets. They asked the alcoholics, *before* they had started to drink from a bottle of 'meths' and were still sober, what they hoped to get out of drinking it. They all said that they hoped to feel better. When the psychologists asked them how they felt *after* drinking the meths, they all reported that they felt worse.

Cheating, dopamine-soaked memories

Alas, what we feel afterwards isn't what addiction allows us to remember. When a craving occurs and the security officer sends the dopamine-laced permission request to the boss's secretary, who then seeks information from the personal memory store, the memories that are pulled out are the ones that are the most soaked in dopamine; distorted or entirely false. Most experiences that are recalled and sent on up to the boss's secretary *never actually happened*.

For instance, a typical memory that might arrive in the folder to help the boss's secretary decide whether Jean has a wonderful time when drinking is "All non-drinkers at that party were boring. They spoilt everything by being timid and strait-laced and looked fed up all the time. Jean, however, after several drinks, was lively and fun, demonstrating her talents and her sophisticated sense of humour." In fact, it is probably the case that the non-drinkers were having interesting, animated conversations and were looking fed up because Jean kept slurring vulgar rubbish at them as she tried to force people to listen to her 'sing' whilst wearing an empty bowl as a hat, and then collapsing into hysterics. As we all know, when sober, there is no one so boring as someone who is drunk!

One smoker even remembers recalling non-smokers as being boring, when she was in the throes of withdrawal symptoms. (Smoking, alone of the addictions, isn't usually associated with a change in mood or behaviour.) The amazing sex that is recalled when contemplating the next compulsive sex session with a stranger bears little relation to the greedy, selfish encounter that actually took place. Indeed, the high that is recalled when remembering any addictive activity is always far more stimulating, exciting and satisfying than it

Memory distortion

MEMORY DISTORTION happens continually, even without the assistance of dopamine. Every time we tell a story about ourselves we 'remint' the memory, adjusting it to the occasion and the people present (so the fish that was caught gets bigger and bigger and our actions to stop a mugger get braver and braver), and it is always the last version of the memory that we recall when we come to tell the tale again, usually embellishing it further in some way. Chance contributions or suggestions from other people – was the fish extremely wriggly and slippery? Was he a very tall man? – can even be incorporated into our own 'memories' of the matter. Indeed, we can never have a truly objective memory of an event that took place, as the original will also be coloured by subsequent experiences and feelings. So we completely edit out the unpleasant, dangerous, painful and selfish elements of an activity and, as this false picture is polished up, our recollection of what really happened becomes permanently changed. This process further increases the power of the cheating, dopamine-soaked memories.

ever actually was (because of the added dopamine). So, with memories like that, is it any wonder that we want a repeat of the 'experience'?

But the addictive high *is* an illusion. We are cheated into selective recall that keeps us trapped – what psychologists term 'euphoric recall', a distorted memory of what really happened. All dopamine ever does is buy a cheap trance state – a way of being 'out of it' for a while; a means of avoiding facing the fact that our true needs aren't being met.

This distorted recall is what makes people think will power is something difficult and painful that they have to summon up to fight temptation. But if we can see indulgence in the

The addictive potential of self-harming

SELF-HARMING behaviour, too, can become addictive due to distorted, dopamine-soaked memories of how the behaviour made the person feel. (There are many reasons that people self-harm, but mostly it is an attempt to cope with extreme emotional distress.) Although it is true that when we are injured the body releases its natural painkillers to help us cope, and that makes us feel calmer, when people become tricked by dopamine-soaked memories, they are likely to recall themselves feeling *more* relieved or *more* at peace after self-harming than was actually the case. The result is that the desire to self-harm, and the expectation of the relief that will be derived from it, become even stronger.

addictive activity for what it really does to us and our lives, then will power is wonderfully easy to apply – an aid instead of an obstacle. Once we realise this, we can recognise other lies that addiction tells us.

More of the lies addiction tells us

How many of the following beliefs or excuses can you identify with?

"It makes me feel good"

But for how long? In reality it is such a short-lived good feeling – if it is even that and not an illusion in the first place. Addiction must be so clever to coax you into believing that it makes you feel good, when so much of the time it makes you feel bad – worrying about the money spent on your addictive activity, the damage done to your health, relationships, career and social life, the knocks to your self-esteem. None of us likes to feel that we are in the grip of something we cannot control. It makes us feel bad, not good.

"It's a way to deal with stress"

No. It is always, ultimately, a *cause* of stress, not a 'magic wand' solution to what is distressing us. For instance, when you smoke your blood pressure goes up, not down. If smoking relieved stress, then smokers as a group would be less stressed than non-smokers. This is self-evidently not the case. All smoking does is to take away the temporary discomfort of wanting a nicotine top up. When smokers stop smoking, this discomfort goes away permanently.

Addictive activity is an attempt to relieve distressing feelings – anxiety, anger, depression etc. – caused by innate emotional needs not being met. It's a way of not dealing with something that needs addressing, such as loneliness, boredom or unexpressed anger. It adds to stress instead of diminishing it. It is far more rewarding to confront the unmet needs in your life, and work out healthy ways to meet them, than to have double the problem – the unmet needs *plus* an addiction.

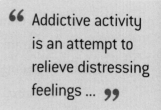

66 Addictive activity is an attempt to relieve distressing feelings ... **99**

"I can't enjoy a social occasion without drinking freely/ eating freely/smoking/taking drugs or whatever"

When you stop and think about this, of course it isn't true! Do young children need addictive substances to help them enjoy parties? Do the people who aren't indulging in these activities seem to be having less interesting conversations or be less likely to dance or join in games? It is a devious illusion that it is the substance we are taking that is enabling us to enjoy an occasion. We would have been enjoying it anyway – and possibly even more so, if spared the guilt or the un-pleasant physical after-effects.

One young woman, who recently came to one of us for help with stopping excessive drinking, recalled an occasion when she had been invited to an evening party in the neighbour-hood. Unexpectedly, she was also invited to an afternoon barbecue on the same day. Knowing her tendency to drink too much, she made the firm resolve that she wouldn't drink at the barbecue, as even she was appalled at the idea of turning up at the evening party already the worse for wear. So she resolutely drank orange juice. At the barbecue she met a number of new people, a couple of whom she really hit it off with. She thoroughly enjoyed the food (usually, once she had a taste for drinking, she didn't bother with food, which, of course, heightened the alcohol's effect on her) and had such a good time that she stayed into the evening and was reluctant to leave and join the second party. Surprised and bolstered by the fact that she had enjoyed herself so much without the aid of alcohol, she decided to have only a couple of drinks at the evening event, instead of her usual six or eight glasses. She later made a point of recalling this memory whenever she needed to strengthen her resolve to stop addictive drinking.

> **She later made a point of recalling this memory whenever she needed to strengthen her resolve.**

Of course, many people do like a drink at social occasions, to help them handle their shyness and lower their inhibitions. Others, whose problem is overeating, may naturally want to enjoy the fine fare that is presented at a celebration. This need not be a problem if the amount they drink or eat is within their control. We are not preaching abstinence; we are urging self-control – volition – and true volition is quite the opposite of addictive activity.

"Smoking makes me less tense/helps me concentrate"

As we have already mentioned, it is a myth that smoking aids concentration, as research has shown that the opposite is true. Similarly, smoking doesn't reduce tension, although it may seem to displace it. If you are anxiously waiting for an important piece of news, smoking is no more helpful as a distraction than pacing the room or playing with worry beads.

"I love the taste"

The taste of cigarettes, alcohol and marijuana initially strikes the palate as disgusting. (All children dislike such substances if they try them.) They are an acquired taste – but one that adults are prepared to acquire because of the associated pleasure that they have been led to expect from them by their peers and the culture in which they were brought up. But many people who first try such substances when they are young have such an unpleasant experience that they choose never to try them again. It isn't natural to 'love the taste' of cigarettes or wine or marijuana, any more than it is natural to love the taste of household cleaning products.

Similarly, while the taste of bread or chocolate or sugar may be enjoyable when taken in small amounts, it is not enjoyable when taken in excessive quantities. Binge eaters often hardly taste what they are eating at all.

"When I feel out of control or stressed, taking drugs makes me feel in control again"

Exactly. It is an illusion, a feeling, not a fact. Taking drugs actually gives people *less* control over their lives. The drug is pulling their strings. Their existence can, for example, become dominated by the need to be secretive, the need to find a way to finance their habit, the physical effort needed to acquire the drug and to use it, to say nothing of the guilt and the social exclusion they may eventually suffer.

"There's no harm in just one"

One doesn't mean one or once, when addiction is talking. It means one after another or again and again.

"I deserve a little pleasure after what I've been through"

Anything that is addictive quickly ceases to be a pleasure. One or two drinks may be a pleasure. A couple of one-hour sessions each week at the gym may be a pleasure. An occasional chocolate bar may be a pleasure. But compulsive over-indulgence is not a pleasure.

"So what if it affects my health? – it's quality of life that matters"

Of course, if we are concerned about our addictive activity, it is the poor quality of our life that worries us! When we realise the extent to which addiction deceives us, quality of life matters very much indeed – we want to recover it, not squander it to addiction.

"So what if it affects my health? After all, I could be hit by a bus tomorrow!"

According to that logic, it is hardly worth getting out of bed and doing anything at all. The odds are that you *won't* be hit by a bus tomorrow. However, the odds are pretty high that your health will be adversely affected, sooner rather than later, by any addictive activity.

"I'll stop tomorrow"

If you are at the point where you know you need to stop your compulsive activity, a clever way that addiction keeps you hooked is to get you to set a date for stopping that is days, weeks or months away. "I'll stop on Monday/the first of next month/the first day of next year." So, in the meantime, you think you'd better get in as much of the addictive activity as possible, as you will never be doing it again. And, "that can't do much harm, can it, seeing as I will be stopping for good?" So, with the deadline looming, you smoke even more cigarettes, or drink even more alcohol and more often, or buy a whole wardrobe of new outfits or drink several more cups of coffee a day or eat whole boxes of chocolate or gamble every night, and so on. And what happens? The day for stopping comes, the boss's secretary ends up persuading the boss to change his mind, and all you've done is upped your addiction levels!

"I can't live without it"

If you were locked up in a cell tomorrow, you would have to manage without 'it', and you would. And, if you follow the approach set out in this book, even that enforced withdrawal would not be a problem. Should you choose instead to experience withdrawal symptoms in their most complete, florid splendour, you would still survive. Everyone can live without addictive activity. The real question is, can you live *with* it?

Jam tomorrow

Remember, addiction doesn't deliver. The good bit is always coming next, after one more drink, one more roll of the dice, one more *haute couture* dress. It just sets up a pattern of craving – a pattern of emotional expectation that is never fulfilled. Jam always tomorrow – but tomorrow never comes.

Logic never cured addiction – but your emotions can

Some people, as mentioned earlier, think that all they need to do to stop being enslaved by their addictive activity is to decide to stop doing it. (You may even have thought this yourself.) In a calm, rational moment, they have looked at the damage the activity is doing to their lives and come to the decision to

> **66** The only thing that instigates behaviour change is emotion. **99**

halt it. This is a bit like the boss saying that smoking is no longer allowed, without thinking through the emotional impact of the decision.

The only thing that ever instigates behaviour change is emotion. Emotion ('stirring up, moving out') is what gives energy to behaviour change. There have to be strong feelings behind the new behaviour, to give it the power to stick. Yes, we need the intellectual realisation about how an addictive activity is destroying our lives. But we need the emotional response – the disgust, shame, guilt and fear about our old activity and the hope, happiness and confidence that arise from our aspirations for beating it – to enable us to pay more than lip service to our decision to quit.

It is only when, in the calm light of reason, you can stand back and look at the expectations you have of your addictive activity, and at what you actually get from it, that you can see the illusion of addiction. When you reach the point where you really feel that your addiction gives you more pain than pleasure (or soon will do), *you just won't want to do it anymore.* Once you truly feel the disgust, the fear, the shame, the pain caused to yourself and to others, you won't want to indulge in that old addictive activity any more than you would want to drink mustard mixed with water. It isn't will power that stops you. It's revulsion!

Exchanging the files

When new information overtakes old information, the memories that we have stored for that subject have to be updated. If you look up 'planet Earth', no current textbook will tell you that it is flat. Similarly, once we recognise that our addiction is disgusting, our old distorted but euphoric memories associated with it have to get corrected and re-edited to include the accurate facts about what our addiction has really done, and is still doing, to us. So, from now on, we have to repeatedly bring to mind the revolting aspects of our addiction so as to undermine the euphoric memories that lied to us and were so well rehearsed in the past.

We also have to program into our memory store new expectations about how wonderful life free from addiction really is. (And it is! No one who has freed themselves from cigarettes, alcohol, heroin, gambling, pornography or over-eating has ever wished to be controlled by those addictions again.)

After the reprogramming, when the boss's secretary gets a message from the security officer, alerting her that another bout of the addictive activity is due, the memories she receives from the memory store are rather different from the one she used to get. The memory store tells her that the addictive activity is not desirable at all, and we will have a much better time without it, so the boss's secretary just bins the whole file, without even bothering the boss. In other words, desire for the addictive activity no longer reaches consciousness at all. And pretty soon, as with any urge that isn't acted on, the instinctive associations with the activity die out; they cease to appear on the control monitor and the security officer doesn't register them either.

That is why withdrawal symptoms are so mild, if you choose them to be so. They are entirely governed by expectation.

An Irish wedding

Joe tested all this out on himself. He was planning to attend a friend's wedding, the sort of occasion where, in Ireland, it is often the convention that guests will drink to excess. That is what is expected at such celebratory occasions. All his life Joe had joined in the spirit of things and invariably had too much to drink, spending the next day with a hangover and the two or three days after that not feeling up to scratch.

So, on this occasion, he said to himself, "Now, Joe, before you go on this binge, which will upset you for days, let's take a look at it. If I'm right about this expectation theory of addiction, the withdrawal symptoms will be very mild if I choose not to take a drink. It will only feel bad if the boss's secretary starts drawing up rosy memories of past Irish weddings and boozing – sprinkling them with a big dose of 'cocaine' to make me feel I want to do all that drinking again."

So he thought about it and realised that, if he wanted to enjoy the wedding without drinking, he had to set up an expectation within himself that *not* drinking would be more enjoyable than drinking. First, he reminded himself of what he usually thought he would get out of drinking at such occasions – an easy way to forget any worries he had and to overcome shyness, and, in the addition, the expectation that something wonderful would happen when he drank. But then he reminded himself that nothing wonderful ever did happen. It was always, elusively, going to be the next drink that did the trick. So one of his positives was really an illusion – a dangerous illusion, because it encour-

> 66 ... he had to set up an expectation that *not* drinking would be more enjoyable. 99

aged more and more drinking, which inevitably resulted in feeling ill and having a horrible hangover the next day.

The illusion of something wonderful happening and the unpleasant consequence of feeling ill for days were the negative expectations he set up about drinking. To make the thought of getting inebriated even more revolting he purposefully recalled occasions in the past when he had drunk too much and subsequently been embarrassed or ashamed at his drunken behaviour. Then he needed some positive expectations about how good it would feel not to drink at the wedding. What a powerful sense of control he would feel, not to be at the mercy of drink! He could discriminate between conversations that were worth having and drunken conversations that weren't worth listening to. He would actually be able to listen to what people were saying and talk intelligently himself. He reminded himself of how children don't need alcohol to enjoy their parties. "Of course, they don't! The human brain, the most intelligent organ in the universe (as far as we know), doesn't need drink to make it happy! It doesn't need poison to overcome a little shyness and enjoy itself!"

He realised that, revising his expectations in this way would have been inconceivable to him only half an hour earlier. After all, the party would be a huge event and not joining in the ritualised, alcoholic indulgence that always accompanied such occasions would be unusual to say the least. But he decided firmly there and then that he would not take a drink at the wedding. At that very moment, he noticed a dryness in his mouth and a furring of his lips. It was the ever-on-duty 'security officer' pattern matching to the notion of drinking and giving him symptoms of withdrawal – and the party hadn't even started yet! But, because Joe was looking at the situation calmly and rationally, he was able to think. "If that's all you can do, it's pathetic!" And the sensation disappeared.

Joe went to the wedding and he didn't drink. And whenever the furring, dry sensation came again, as it did a few times, he just called up his negative expectations of drinking and his positive expectations of not drinking, and the sensation vanished once again. He didn't have a great battle in his brain. He experienced, instead, a surge of pleasure in the fact that he was in control and making a genuine choice not to drink. He then went on to try this out on other social occasions and thoroughly enjoyed staying sober at them too.

> " He experienced a surge of pleasure from being in control and making a genuine choice ... "

This is the testing moment

When you *truly* perceive that the negative aspects of addiction outweigh the pleasure, and see how harmful it is, you will want to stop your addictive activity.

But if you don't stop right now or set a date for stopping/cutting down that is in the very near future, you are not letting your new insight touch you emotionally.

When you fully *feel* the illusion of addiction, stopping will be relatively easy. The only difficult part in overcoming an addiction is creating enough space inside yourself to receive the insight and give it emotional commitment – a strong expectation that addiction will bring misery and that freedom from it will open the way to true satisfaction and joy.

> 66 When you fully *feel* the illusion of addiction stopping will be relatively easy. 99

Remember, addiction has hijacked your expectation circuitry, so it is trying as hard as it can to keep you hooked with unrealistic expectations. But you can reclaim that circuitry just by imposing a different set of expectations on it, ones that reveal the lure of addiction to be nothing more than a false bait – with you as the fish hooked on the end of the line.

Once anyone truly sees how addiction is hurting them, they will want to stop, even if they are old or ill and haven't got much time left to them. This is because it is absolutely wonderful, not painful, to feel the volition that comes from taking control (instead of being controlled), however late in the day.

In the next section, we will show you how to make such a shift of expectations, if you haven't already now done so. And then we will show you ways to use your innate resources to embed those new expectations firmly in your heart and mind. There is nothing more to it than that.

PART 2

Overcoming addiction

'*I*F A good thing comes your way, seize it!' says the old proverb. Having read the first section of this book you are now in a much stronger position to tackle your own addiction – whatever it is. You now know the processes it uses to trick you and how these can be overcome.

Since first discussing these ideas with other therapists and using them in therapy, we have helped many people to take back control of their lives and overcome their compulsions. So now, to help you further, we are going to explain the human givens approach to behaviour change. It will help you to see that giving up an addictive activity really is much easier than you previously thought – if you absorb the necessary information, put together the right package of skills and go about it in the right way.

The human givens

As you may have noticed, we have already mentioned the term 'human givens' a few times. Now we want to look at what this means in more depth.

To live successful and fulfilled lives we all need to have certain basic needs met and, to help us get them met, nature gave us inherent abilities and skills (innate resources). Because all babies come into the world with these needs and resources, we call them human givens. They are a form of knowledge programmed into us – our natural genetic inheritance.

We all accept that we need food, water, sufficient sleep, warmth and shelter from the elements in order to survive – these are basic 'givens'. But there are many other needs, *emotional* rather than *physical*, which are equally crucial for our well-being – and, sometimes, even for survival too. These include the needs for:

- security: a sense of being safe, which enables us to lead our lives without undue fear

- volition: a sense of autonomy and control over our lives

- attention: receiving it from others, but also giving it

- emotional connection to other people: friendship, love, intimacy, fun

- connection to the wider community: being part of something larger than ourselves

The three essential steps to beating addiction

Every successful addiction plan has the following three key elements, which are all fully explained and illustrated throughout this section of the book.

1. **Knock out the positive expectations** that addiction feeds us with

2. **Revamp your lifestyle** to get your needs met more successfully

3. **Anticipate high risk situations** and have a range of coping strategies in place.

– privacy: to reflect

– a sense of status: being accepted and valued in the different social groups we belong to

– a sense of our own competence and achievements: which ensures we don't suffer from 'low self-esteem'

– a sense of meaning and purpose: which comes from doing things that mentally and/or physically stretch us.

Nature programmed each one of us with these needs while we were in the womb, along with an 'instruction', once we were in the world, to seek out situations that would satisfy them. When our innate needs are met in a balanced way, we are mentally healthy.

Moreover, to help us find ways to meet our needs, nature has given us a wealth of resources, such as:

– the ability to add new knowledge to innate knowledge: to learn and remember

– the ability to build rapport, empathise and connect with others

– a powerful imagination

– the ability to think things out, analyse, plan and adapt

– the ability to understand the world unconsciously: through pattern matching

– the ability to step back into our 'observing self' (our self-awareness), and be objective.

These needs and resources together – the human givens – are in-built patterns, or biological templates, which direct our actions and responses.

If any of our needs are seriously unmet, or any of our innate resources are damaged, missing or used incorrectly (whether we realise it or not), we suffer mental distress – becoming anxious, angry or depressed, which are nature's powerful signals for telling us to get back on track.

It is crucial to understand this: when essential needs are not being met in our lives we are at greatest risk of embarking on unhealthy activities that may, initially, mask our distress but that later become addictive. For example, experimenting with addictive drugs mainly occurs when people are young – a time when they feel extremely insecure and worry about concerns such as peer group rejection, the ability to attract and keep a partner, or how they are going to support themselves in the world.

Sometimes people turn to drink or drugs or other addictive behaviours as 'self-medication', to try and mask the psychological distress caused by having a troubled family background, suffering chronic illness or being bullied, or to relieve the symptoms that result from experiencing trauma. In other cases people who are not being stretched in their lives seek to give themselves the good feelings artificially – the 'buzz' generated by addictive experiences – that they would otherwise have experienced naturally, through absorbing, worthwhile activities and achievements.

> " When our essential needs are not being met we are at greatest risk of embarking on unhealthy activities ... "

Human givens therapists working with addiction look to see which important needs are unmet in people's lives and/or which of their innate resources are either not being used at all or are being used incorrectly. We then help a person build up effective ways to meet their needs, at the same time as they are handling their addiction. These are the techniques we are going to share with you now.

Questions to ask yourself

A good place to start is to take a close look at your addiction and the part that it plays in your life. In a calm moment, when you have some time, we suggest you take a piece of paper and a pen, sit back and reflect. If you have already taken the decision to quit and feel fully emotionally committed to your decision, your list will be an aid to your motivation. If you are still ambivalent, the process of answering these questions may help you tip the balance towards change.*

1. What does addiction do for me?

You won't pursue a behaviour that threatens your health and your life unless you believe that it also offers something that you value highly. We are not trying to make you deny the positives of your addictive experience, but to weigh them up. Take a moment to think about:

- *how and why you started*
- *what you enjoyed about it*
- *how your usage has changed over time* (have you upped the amount of time you spend engaged in your problematic activity?)

---

* We would like to acknowledge here the pioneering work of William R. Miller and Stephen Rollnick, who developed the technique known as motivational interviewing, on which these questions are based.

- *what it is you like about it now*
- *what good experiences you've had with it*
- *whether you enjoy it as much now as you used to do*
- *what makes you want to do it* (for instance associations with certain event, places, people, times or emotional states)
- *what goes through your mind when you <u>really</u> want to do it*
- *what you perceive that it gives you* (for instance confidence, excitement, relief from boredom or anxiety).

2. Do I have any concerns about my addiction?

Clearly, although there have been many aspects of the addictive activity that you have found positive and desirable, you also have some considerable concerns or you wouldn't be reading this book. Think about:

- *any negative effects on your physical health* (this might include not just disease, or the risk of disease, but effects such as not eating, sleeping or exercising properly)
- *any negative effects on your relationships with family and friends* (this might include reduced closeness, more arguments, less time spent with people you care about, lies you may have to tell them, or embarrassing and irresponsible things you have said or done 'under the influence')
- *any negative effects on your emotional health* (for instance

feeling jittery or depressed if you can't get to engage in your addictive activity, increased anxiety and stress, guilt feelings, and unhappiness caused by the adverse effects on relationships)

- *any negative effects on your work life* (for instance failing to perform at your optimum level, less interest in your job/home responsibilities, loss of ambition or drive)

- *any negative effects on your social life* (for instance, giving up leisure activities you used to enjoy, ceasing to see so much of people who don't share your addiction, avoiding doing things or going to places where you cannot carry out your addictive activity)

- *any negative effects on your financial position* (for instance, reducing your earning power if your compulsive activity takes a lot of time, or not providing adequately for your needs or those of others you are responsible for, if it costs a lot of money. Perhaps you are even in serious debt)

- *any illegal activities you might feel compelled to carry out* (for instance, theft, shoplifting, burglary and prostitution, to fund your addiction. Drugs and alcohol are key factors in many non-violent crimes. But there are also strong associations between alcohol consumption and violent crime, particularly among young males aged between 15 and 25. Often the buzz people get out of committing criminal acts becomes addictive in itself)

- *any negative effects on your self-esteem* (for instance, does the activity make you feel better or worse about yourself, the way you live your life, your sense of autonomy and what you make of your talents and abilities?)

3. What concerns might other people have about my addictive activity?

Even if, in the above section, there are some areas in which you do not have concerns, there might be people in your life, at home or at work, who do have concerns about the effects of your behaviour, whether or not you agree with them.

Take a moment now to list for yourself who they are and any concerns they have about:

- *your health*
- *your relationship with them*
- *the amount of time you spend on your addictive activity*
- *the amount of time you spend with them*
- *changes in your behaviour and attitude*
- *the amount of attention you pay to your work*
- *the amount of attention you pay to your family*
- *the financial situation you are in.*

4. What are my hopes for the future?

Think realistically about all the things you have worked towards or have hoped would happen. For instance:

- *promotion at work to a particular level*
- *success in a chosen field*
- *the chance to study for a new career*
- *the chance to learn a particular new skill or develop an existing talent*
- *building a successful business*
- *meeting a special partner and developing a happy relationship*
- *nurturing an already valued relationship*
- *living according to the tenets of a religious faith*
- *buying a flat, a house or a bigger house*
- *caring for, or improving, your home*
- *having children*
- *giving your children the best chances in life*
- *spending time with grandchildren*
- *seeing more of the world, perhaps going on a dream holiday*
- *helping others through, for instance, local politics or community work.*

5. Might my addictive activity get in the way?

- *Has your compulsive habit prevented you from achieving anything you had wanted to do?*

- *If not, so far, is it possible that, in the future, it might prevent you from achieving what you want to do in your life. Look back at your 'hopes for the future' list and your 'concerns' list to help you answer this question.*

For instance, Ida had planned early retirement so that she could spend extended periods of time with her daughter, son-in-law and new baby grandson, who live in a different country. But she is worried that the health consequences of her smoking are now catching up with her (she has chronic bronchitis) and will leave her too ill to travel to see them – or even that she'll die before being able to see them at all.

Angus is aware that his cocaine habit, which started because most of his city bank colleagues 'did cocaine', is now taking over his life, threatening his career prospects and his ability to pay his large mortgage. His fiancée doesn't approve of his habit so he keeps pretending he has stopped. This means telling her ever more complicated lies and, unsurprisingly, as a result they are growing apart.

6. How would I like things to be different?

- *What would you like to be able to change, so that you can achieve your hopes for the future?*

- *What would be the beneficial effects of stopping or cutting down your addictive activity?*

- *How might you feel physically, if you stopped or cut down?*

- *How would you feel about yourself, if you stopped or cut down?*

Avoid giving addiction a chance

Having answered all these questions as honestly as you can, remember that addiction lies to you. If your answers to the questions in sections 2–6 take up more space, when added together, than your answers to the questions in section 1, it seems that, on balance, you would rather not be stuck in your addictive activity. Of course, your answers to the questions in section 1 reflect what you think addiction does for you, otherwise you wouldn't engage in it. But, if your concerns are outweighing the perceived positives, you might want to study and understand your addiction a bit more deeply. For instance, you might want to look in a bit more depth at what you have written about the good things that addiction does for you.

Perhaps you have written that having a drink or a cigarette gives you confidence when you are in a social situation. But are you sure that you must have a drink or a cigarette to feel confident? Think of all the other occasions when you can't have a drink or a cigarette – at work, perhaps? Many of these occasions will be 'social', in that you are mixing with and relating to other people, often people you don't know well or at all? Do you never ever feel confident then?

Apply this kind of questioning to the statements you have written about your own addictive activity.

Never argue with addiction

If, however, you find yourself resisting the idea of questioning the good aspects of your addiction, put the list away and come back to it another time. You don't ever want to argue with addiction. That only empowers it. As we said earlier, your addiction is as clever as you are. It enlists your emotions, to make you want to have it or do it. And, as any highly emotionally aroused, screaming toddler in a toy store knows, when you want it, you *want* it! You'll find a million ways to argue against any reason you are given for not having it.

So, be aware, if you aren't ready to see what addiction is really doing to you and you find yourself putting up arguments to defend it, the defences will be coming from the emotionally immature, but deviously clever toddler that is your addiction, not the calm, rational adult that is your intelligent mind. Remember, *you are not your addiction.*

If, however, you have fully recognised just how much the pain and misery of addiction outweigh its perceived positives, then your heart and mind are cooperating, and you are halfway to success.

The chest X-ray that tipped the balance

One woman we were told of had smoked for 37 years – 40 cigarettes a day for at least 25 of them – and struggled terribly to give up smoking. She tried innumerable times to stop and never managed to last even a single day without a cigarette. Routinely, she would be in a screaming panicky state long before evening. Sometimes she made attempts to cut down, deciding to allow herself a cigarette on the hour – one at 9 am, one at 10 am and so on. By 10.30 am, she would already be on the 3 pm cigarette! This woman was kept awake at night by her fear of lung cancer, emphysema, mouth cancer and heart disease, but she still couldn't kick the habit. Then, while abroad, staying with her sister, she had an asthma attack for the first time in her life. She was rushed to her sister's doctor, who took X-rays. Studying them, he asked her, "How old are you?"

"Fifty-four," she replied.

He shook his head in disbelief. "This is the chest of a 74-year-old woman," he told her.

For the first time, in no uncertain terms, she had been given tangible proof of the damage smoking was doing to her body and her life. It was

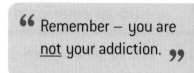

Remember – you are not your addiction.

enough to tip the scales completely against her addiction. This woman who had convinced herself that she couldn't think or function without a cigarette stopped smoking immediately and has never had a cigarette since.

It is a story we hear all the time. For some people it may take a heart attack to convince them to stop smoking, drinking, overeating and getting no exercise. For some, it is having a child and becoming responsible for another life, with all the hands-on physical and emotional requirements that brings, that puts an end to the desire to pursue a destructive addictive activity. But you don't *have* to wait until some potentially fatal disaster or momentous event occurs to muster the power to make changes.

The greater expectation you have of fulfilment in your life *without* the addictive activity, the easier it will be to stop. So now we want you to look at any areas in your life where important emotional needs are not being met.

Do an emotional 'needs audit' on yourself

If people's lives are going well, they do not spiral down into addiction. People become entrapped by addictive activities only when particular circumstances prevent their emotional needs from being met or they unwittingly misuse innate resources.

Think back to when you were first aware that your problem activity was becoming addictive and see if you can recall what was happening in your life at the time. Was anything upsetting or concerning you? Had some significant change occurred in your life – for instance, the end of a relationship, the death of someone close, a move to somewhere new, the loss of a job, the birth of a baby, the development of a health problem? Often, although we may be introduced to an activity, such as smoking, drinking, exercising or shopping, on a fun occasion, it is when things go adrift in our lives that we increase our indulgence in that activity and become reliant on it, to fill the gap.

To handle addiction with the greatest chance of success, you need to identify clearly what is not going right in your life at the moment, so that you can take some practical steps to deal with it. Take some time when you can be calm and not likely to be disturbed, and go through the list of needs below one by one. Note down any areas where you are aware your needs are not being satisfyingly met.

(We have already mentioned that smoking is slightly different from other addictions, because it can be carried on alongside your usual activities. But the more fulfilled you are in your life, the easier it will be for you to kick the habit. So completing the emotional needs audit should benefit smokers too.)

Try to be as honest and probing as you can, when answering the following questions. (Sometimes the delusional trance state of addiction makes it hard to see what is really true.) You will be providing yourself with information that you need to make use of in your journey out of addiction. For instance, you may realise that your needs for intimacy or social connection are not being met satisfyingly, and that you need to take steps to change this.

Do you feel safe?

For instance, do you feel comfortable about your work situation or do you feel distrustful of any colleagues or your boss? Do you feel unsafe at home or with a particular relationship you have with someone? Are your parents splitting up? Do you find social occasions, where you don't know anyone, difficult to handle? Are you being bullied? Have you been the victim of violence? Is your livelihood or home at risk? Do you indulge in your addictive activity to push away worries?

A past experience of trauma is a common cause of insecurity and lack of trust. Although the horrific event – for instance an assault, a rape, sexual or physical abuse as a child, escaping fire, nearly drowning or being the victim in a road, rail or air accident – is in the past, it can still have an impact on your actions and reactions today, if the experience was emotionally overwhelming at the time. Addictive behaviour can be used, consciously or unconsciously, as a means of pushing away the flashbacks and nightmares that may keep occurring, or of avoiding having to face feared situations that recall the traumatic event. For instance, someone who has been raped or otherwise sexually abused may avoid intimate relationships and substitute the buzz of an addiction for the good feelings they would normally get within an intimate relationship.

> 66 Addictive behaviour can be used, consciously or unconsciously, to push away symptoms of trauma ... 99

There is a simple psychological technique for resolving post-traumatic stress (PTSD) which human givens therapists are trained to use (details of this are given on pages 198–9). It recodes the traumatic memory as a low-arousal memory – a highly unpleasant memory but one that doesn't arouse strong emotions and has no bearing on today. It is out-of-control strong emotions, aroused at the merest reminder of the horrible event or events, that keep the trauma alive and allow it to impinge on your present-day life.

Do you have people in your life who are important to you and to whom you are important?

Do those relationships fulfil your needs for intimacy? Do you feel understood? Have you found yourself withdrawing more and more from those people, as a result of your addictive activity? Have you lost touch with friends or stopped seeing them lately? Is there at least one person with whom you can be yourself, have fun and share your joys and anxieties? Or have you experienced loss? For instance, are you still mourning a serious relationship that ended a while ago or still grieving for someone who has died?

Do you have wider connections?

For instance, do you know people other than close family and close friends? Do you help others, such as elderly neighbours, or are you involved in voluntary work of any kind? Do you go regularly to a church or other religious institution? Are you involved with any neighbourhood schemes or local politics or do you participate in any community activities, such as serving on a parish council, or supporting a local football team, or taking part in a drama group, book group or aerobics class? Does your work connect you with many other people? Have you ceased to participate in regular activities because of a particular changed circumstance, such as unemployment, a newborn baby or a disability or chronic illness? Have you withdrawn from such activities the more you have indulged in your addictive activity?

Are you comfortable with your status in society?

For instance, do you feel good about the way you see yourself and the way you think that other people view you? Do you feel suitably rewarded or appreciated for what you do? Are your achievements acknowledged fairly by others? Do you feel you should have achieved more, or that others have done better than you? Do you feel you fit in? Do you feel inferior or hostile to others or often jealous of them? Do you yearn for what you haven't got?

Do you have a sense of competence and achievement?

For instance, on balance, are you doing what you want to do with your life or have your interests developed in a different direction? Do you have skills that you feel totally competent employing? (People who feel incompetent a lot, or all, of the time feel badly about themselves and may be described as having 'low self-esteem'.) Do you enjoy the way you spend your time and feel satisfyingly stretched by it? Or do you feel you have taken on more than you can comfortably manage and the quality of what you do has deteriorated? Do you feel unsatisfied, not challenged, stuck or bored, perhaps because there is nothing further you can achieve at work or your children have grown up and left home? Do you resort to the addictive activity if you can't see a way out of a problem or if you become frustrated? Does all of your satisfaction come from your addictive activity?

Do you have a sense of autonomy and control?

For instance, do you feel you have sufficient responsibility in your work life or too little or too much? Do you have the power to take the responsibility for important decisions in many aspects of your life? Does someone you know have too much influence or power over you? Have you recently lost your sense of control, perhaps because of unexpected illness or the arrival of a new person at work or a baby at home or the introduction into your life of difficult in-laws? Do you feel you should be able to control things that, in fact, you can't control – such as how hard your children study – and feel a failure when you can't? Do you feel controlled by your addiction?

How healthily are your attention needs being met?

We all need to receive and give attention. But attention is a form of nutrition and, like food, we need the right kind, in the right amount, at the right time. Do you spend too much time alone? Do other people make too many demands of your time, wanting to see you more often than you want to see them, and sapping your energy in the process? Or do you feel shy and therefore stay in the background at social occasions?

Do you feel overshadowed by someone you spend time with, who always seems to grab the attention in public? When you engage in your addictive activity, do you enjoy the attention you give to and get from other people who share it? Do you engage in the activity primarily in an attempt to meet your needs for attention? How much sincere attention do you give to other people? Do you get attention by having others close to you worry about your addiction?

Do you have a sense of meaning and purpose in your life?

For instance, are there people you know who need you in their lives – and do you meet that need? Do you have activities that interest and continue to challenge you? (This may be particularly important if you are retired from work and have a large gap in your life to fill productively. You need to stretch yourself mentally and physically and set realistic goals for yourself, whatever age you are.) Do you have a philosophy or approach to life that helps you see life as intrinsically meaningful? Do you have a commitment to something bigger than yourself: a cause, a sport, a religion, a school, a community activity or political campaign? Is your addictive activity turning you inward and draining away the sense that your life is meaningful? (As we've said, true meaning derives from being stretched to engage more with the world.)

How well are your emotional needs being met?

YOU MIGHT like to use this checklist when carrying out your own emotional needs audit. Rate, in your judgement, how well the following emotional needs are being met in your life now, on a scale of one to seven (where 1 means not met at all, and 7 means being very well met).

- Do you feel secure – in your home life?
  - in your work life?
  - in your environment?
- Do you feel you receive enough attention?
- Do you think you give other people enough attention?
- Do you feel in control of your life most of the time?
- Do you feel part of the wider community?
- Can you obtain privacy when you need to?
- Do you have at least one close friend?
- Do you have an intimate relationship in your life (i.e. you are totally physically and emotionally accepted for who you are by at least one person)?
- Do you feel an emotional connection to others?
- Do you have a status in life (whatever it may be) that you value and that is acknowledged?
- Are you achieving things in your life that you are proud of?
- Do you feel competent in at least one major area of your life?
- Are you mentally and/or physically stretched in ways which give you a sense of meaning and purpose?

If you have scored any need at 3 or less, this is likely to be a major stressor for you.

Even if you have scored only one need very low, it can be enough of a problem to have a serious, adverse effect on your life, which could lead to addictive behaviour.

Self-esteem

Low self-esteem – the feeling of being 'rubbish' – is suffered by many people with addictive behaviours, although they may use their addiction to hide the fact that they don't feel good about themselves and their place in the world. It may occur as a result of being told when young that we were unlovable, worthless, bad, unwanted or stupid, and we took in those false messages about ourselves. Sometimes we may over-react to negative events that happen to us (such as losing a job or being left by a lover) and our strong emotions reduce us to black-and-white thinking – one thing went wrong, so *everything* is hopeless – and we write ourselves off as worthless beings. When people feel that they are not valued they may immerse themselves in an addictive activity.

On the other hand, they may have slipped into addiction in response to temporary setbacks in their lives – someone may be let down by a partner, so go to a bar to seek sex with a stranger or go to a shop to buy designer clothes or expensive gadgets, to try to feel that they are worthy of attention. Gradually, as the addictive activity takes hold and they no longer feel in control of their lives, they suffer a major blow to their self-esteem.

Self-esteem is a buzz term with psychologists and self-help experts – 'having it' is seen as vital for mental health – but it isn't actually something you have to aim for at all. Positive feelings about yourself emerge naturally when you engage with life in a meaningful way. When you master new skills and develop new competencies and feel sure of the support of good friends and the love of people close to you, self-esteem is yours. When we engage in activities that truly have value to us, and when ▶

Put back some perspective

You may find, when you look hard, that many parts of your life are (or could be) working well, but you don't acknowledge them or make the most of them, because your preoccupation with the addiction has left you uninterested in them. Or you may have turned to an addiction because just one aspect of your life went wrong, and have ended up with knock-on effects. For instance, a man who has a satisfying job and a meaningful social world may turn to drink after being left by a lover, and gradually the drinking may ruin the parts of his life that were running smoothly and enjoyably

we are helping and serving others, that is when we feel best about who we are. In other words, the more you focus outwards, away from your addiction, the better you will feel about yourself and the more free of the addiction.

High self-esteem is not the opposite of low self-esteem, and it is not something to strive for. As people have pointed out for thousands of years, esteeming the self is damaging. Those with high self-esteem tend to be selfish and greedy and take little account of other people's feelings and opinions.

Self-esteem goes up and down. If you find yourself thinking a lot about your addictive activity and toying with 'just once more', it is a signal that something isn't right in your personal life or at work – something that you need to address rather than avoid by indulging in the addictive activity.

before. A young woman, feeling low because she hasn't a boyfriend, may start extreme dieting or extreme exercising after hearing a disparaging comment about her personal appearance from a 'friend', and then, as the addiction develops, gradually withdraw more and more from social activities with her true friends.

When you become obsessed with a certain substance or activity, it may seem to push out the need for all others – and that is what you are trying to get back in perspective here.

Caroline's story

Caroline was married to a businessman and didn't have to work for a living. Her husband Eric's business had been UK-based, and she had been deeply involved with it until it expanded. Eric then appointed someone full time to perform the role that he and Caroline had shared together and was now abroad a great deal of the time, promoting his business internationally. Because they had no children, she spent a great deal of time alone.

As a result, Caroline became a compulsive shopper, running up frighteningly large debts on her credit cards but still feeling impelled to make trips to top designer shops to try on the most expensive new outfits. She continually came home with bags of clothing, most of which she never wore. She wasn't even interested, half the time, in hanging them up in her wardrobe.

But, when she carried out the emotional needs audit, she realised that it wasn't really the clothes that she wanted; it was the buzz she got from the attention the shop assistants gave her. These were elegant women who were knowledgeable about fashion and style and she revelled in having them focus on her, giving her their exclusive attention, admiring her choices, offering advice, deciding what suited her best.

Now Caroline could finally face the fact that she was deeply lonely and had lost her sense of purpose, once her role in the business ended. She realised she would feel much better about herself if she developed some skills and followed pursuits that were truly worthy of approval. As well as broadening her social life, so that she wasn't so dependent on her husband's being around, she became involved in fundraising for a local charity – and used her knowledge of fashion to organise fun fashion shows.

Set your goals

If you have now realised what is missing in your life, you can set goals that will best help you overcome your addictive activity. We have provided a blank box (overleaf) for you to use to record them in.

Your goals should be of two kinds. The first type should concern your *intentions* about your addictive activity: the second should be about the *actions* you plan to take to fill the void in your life. Remember, addiction takes up an enormous amount of time, in our thinking as well as our actions. You need to fill that time in positive ways that enable you to restore the balance to your life by ensuring you get your emotional needs met more effectively.

In this section, we are *only* concerned with your goals. But don't worry, we will move on later to the strategies we recommend that you use to help you achieve them.

■ MY GOALS

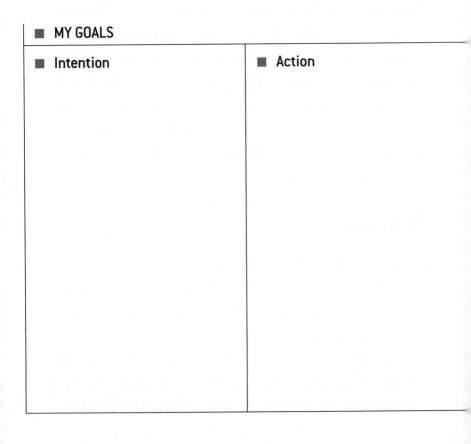

■ Intention	■ Action

Goal 1. Stopping or cutting down?

It is crucial that you choose a goal you can work with. You need to decide a goal that you feel comfortable aiming for and that is realistic for you to expect to achieve.

Cutting down

Clearly, the nature of the compulsive activity you want to deal with will determine, in some cases, whether you consider stopping altogether or cutting down. For instance, if you work for too many hours, shop or eat to excess, your goal clearly is to cut down. The decision for you is how much you want to cut down by.

You do not have to do it all in one go. But your eventual aim should be that you are not performing the activity compulsively any more.

Remember, too, that your second set of goals – meeting your needs more healthily – will itself help you deal with withdrawal from your addiction.

Be specific

If you are a workaholic, do not set a goal to 'work less'. That's too vague. You need to specify exactly how much less and be very concrete in your plans. You might decide, for instance, if you routinely arrive at the office at 7 am and don't leave till 9 pm, that you will arrive at the same time but leave two hours earlier for a month. Then, gradually, over a period of a further month, cut back until you are leaving at 5.30 pm. Then, the next month, start arriving 10 minutes later each day, until you are regularly arriving at 9 am. You might decide, from the start, to take no work home or else set a limit (for instance, one hour) and perhaps work to cut that back to zero over an appropriate period. Whilst doing this you would also need to be realistic and flexible about genuine deadlines that you are reasonably required to meet, which might require occasional longer hours. But otherwise stick to your plan.

Similarly, if overeating is your problem, don't just propose to 'eat less'. Decide exactly how much less. Perhaps your initial goal will be not to eat anything after 8 pm. Or to eat only one bar of chocolate a day, if you routinely eat four. Or else you might decide to have just one helping of any course at a meal. Over a timeframe that is manageable for you, and that you therefore feel optimistic about maintaining, set further goals for reduction – perhaps to cut down by a specified amount on all unhealthy food and to increase by a specific amount your intake of healthy ones. If you are specific, you have a clear measure by which you can judge your success and motivate yourself further.

> **If you are specific, you have a clear measure by which you can judge your success ...**

Be realistic

For other kinds of addictive activity, which can be stopped completely, try to think through, before you commit yourself to your goal, whether cutting down is actually a realistic option for you. Are you choosing it because you can't face life without your addictive activity? If so, it may be that you aren't yet fully emotionally committed to dealing with the addictive element of your compulsive activity, and your goal will be all the harder to achieve. (Remember the woman who tried to have one cigarette an hour and ended up half a day ahead of herself!) But it might well be the case that, thinking it through rationally, you have decided you *could* enjoy just one cigarette, after a meal at night, and wish to maintain only that one. (But this will only work if you don't spend all day thinking about and wishing for the time for that one cigarette!)

You may be successful in the choice to cut down, rather than stop, an activity if other needs are being met while you are engaging in it. For instance, some people who have previously drunk too much still want to go to the pub to enjoy time with their friends, so are prepared to have just two pints of beer that will last them the evening, and go to the pub just one night a week instead of six. Very many heavy coffee drinkers choose successfully to cut down rather than stop, because one cup at breakfast is associated with pleasure, whereas the other six were failed attempts to cope with anxiety or lack of concentration. And people who have been addicted to sex with strangers find their sexual needs are more satisfyingly fulfilled in the context of a meaningful relationship.

Stopping altogether

If your addiction doesn't also involve an activity that is essential or healthy in moderate amounts, you may find it easier to contemplate stopping altogether rather than cutting down. If you switch your expectation of pleasure to one of pain, whenever you experience a desire to indulge, you know that your withdrawal messages will be mild and that, in due course, they will cease to reach consciousness at all. You will be free of the addiction entirely, rather than having to manage it.

Consider switching course, if necessary

Many people we have worked with have started by choosing to cut down on their activity and then, later, they have decided of their own accord to stop altogether. Although they had originally felt they would like to indulge a little, their successful cutting down led them to lose all of their interest in the activity. Others decide to stop because they find cutting down harder and less satisfying than they had thought it would be. They had found themselves continuing to dwell on the desire to perform the activity, or else desiring to indulge in it more frequently, thus setting up a battle inside themselves instead of working with their will.

So, think through carefully what you want to achieve and what, realistically, you think you can achieve, when you set your goal. If, having set it, you find the choice you made doesn't suit you, you can decide to switch from abstinence to control, or from control to abstinence. Switching isn't failure. It is all part of the process of putting together the package of skills that you can use to achieve the outcome that works for *you*.

Goal 2. Revamp your lifestyle

This is the time to look back at the notes you made about any significant needs that are currently unmet in your life.

Make social contact

Most people who become addicted to a substance or activity (with some exceptions, such as cigarettes and coffee) tend to withdraw increasingly from other activities that they used to enjoy and from pastimes that involve people who don't share their addiction. But even cigarette smokers and coffee drinkers may have upped their consumption because they are spending too much time alone. If any of this is the case for you, one of your goals should address the need to re-establish contact with people and activities that are not associated with the addictive one.

However, you don't just have to do something you used to enjoy before, you could decide to try something entirely fresh

– or even do both. You might decide to contact old friends or make new ones. (However, if you have always found it hard to form relationships with other people, you may benefit from working with a therapist to develop social skills that perhaps you didn't have the opportunity to learn when you were younger. These can be learned at any age, even by the very shy, and can continually improve with practice.)

Take a moment to consider which of the following ideas for creating a healthier social life would be most appropriate for you:

- call a friend whom you have been meaning to call for ages and suggest you get together

- go out for a walk or a meal with your partner

- take your children to the park, and join in their games

- if childcare is an issue, suggest a babysitting swap with someone you trust who has children, so that you can go out for the evening

- invite a friend, or a couple of friends, for a meal at your house

- take up an activity again that you used to enjoy, such as tennis, swimming, going to art classes, listening to live music, dancing, joining a gardening club or amateur dramatics

- walk your dog with a neighbour or go along when the neighbour takes their dog

- suggest a coffee or a drink after work with colleagues (if neither is your addictive activity)
- go to the cinema or theatre with a friend or partner
- book a holiday where you will meet new people and explore new places
- join a dating agency
- decide on a charity you would like to help and make sure this involves your being in direct contact with people – for instance, visiting at an old people's home, helping disabled children, serving hot food at a soup kitchen for homeless people
- join an evening class that interests you
- go on an activity weekend, where you can meet new people.

Decide on one or two of these sorts of strategies, to start with. They should help you meet your needs for emotional and social connection. Make sure you are doing something that benefits others as well as yourself, as this will raise your self-esteem and make you feel much more positive about yourself.

Start small

Other unmet needs may require you to take a deeper look at your life and explore or plan carefully for change. It is a good idea to list your options if you are no longer happy with work or a relationship and then discuss them with someone whose opinion you trust. Make sure, though, that you start with small steps, rather than rushing to change everything at once. Perhaps an appropriate first goal might be to research alternative areas of employment or look into the practicalities of mending or ending a problematic relationship. If you tend to resort to your addictive activity when you get angry and frustrated or when you can't resolve a difficulty, you may need to learn more effective problem-solving, assertiveness or anger management skills. (These are things a counsellor can help you with or that you can learn on courses or from self-help books.)

> ... take up healthier ways to fill any void in your life ...

Sometimes people slip into addiction because they are stuck in extremely difficult circumstances, where the needs of others must be taken into account as well as their own, and they don't know what to do for the best. Feeling incapable of taking a decision, they resort to alcohol, overeating, anorexia or some other addiction. But sometimes the right thing to do is not to take a life-changing decision, if the change might bring with it just as many problems. At such times, you may need to wait until something else happens that makes your path clear to you. Sooner or later, *everything* changes. In the meantime, you don't need addiction to help you deal with your circumstances. Apply the strategies we suggest in this book and take up healthier ways to fill any void in your life –

for instance, find new ways to be active, keep productively busy, spend time with people you care for, and eat properly.

Techniques to help you reach your goals

We are now going to describe a number of effective techniques that, along with the information you now have, will help you reach your goal of overcoming addiction. We suggest you make use of them all. They aren't difficult to do. They all make use of our innate resources, so you will be working *with* your nature, not fighting against it. And the more you apply these techniques, the easier and the more painless your passage out of addiction will be.

Learn how to relax yourself

Think for a moment about how you feel when you want to engage in your addictive activity but, for some reason, are unable to. You probably find you become highly aroused, perhaps anxious, jittery, consumed with the desire to satisfy your impulse and unable to concentrate on very much else. When this happens you are locked into your 'emotional brain'. And when your emotions are ruling the show, rational thinking doesn't get a look in. (If it were otherwise, as we've said before, people wouldn't contemplate rushing out in bad weather at the dead of night to purchase new supplies of an addictive substance.)

When strong emotions are in charge, they stop us from thinking clearly. Everything is reduced to all-or-nothing emotional terms. "I must have it!" "I can't live without it!" "I can't last another second!" "It's the most wonderful thing in the world!"

Addiction is a strong adversary, but only if you let it take over the reins and have emotional power. When you first start quitting, you will feel mild withdrawal symptoms but it is only by being in a calm state that you will be able to prevent the boss's secretary from drawing up the wrong files from the memory stores – the pleasant, dopamine-soaked illusory memories and associations with your addictive activity.

Only when calm can you choose to let all the real facts come to mind – the negative effects on your health, lifestyle, finances, work performance and so on. So learning to calm yourself through relaxation is essential. One of the first things human givens therapists do is to calm down people who are in an emotionally aroused state, and then teach them how to do this for themselves.

> ❝ Addiction is a strong adversary – but only if you let it have emotional power. ❞

You may think, especially if you use your addictive activity to calm yourself down, that you could never possibly relax without it. However, we haven't come across anyone who couldn't be helped to relax naturally, at least for a while, even people who are actively resistant. It is normal for the body to want relief from the highly unnatural state of unrelenting emotional arousal. A short period of calm is a wonderful gift to give yourself. It will show you, through the very experience of changes you can induce in your own body, that things *can* be different; you *can* make changes happen.

> 66 ... things *can* be different; you *can* make changes happen. 99

Once you become familiar with how relaxation feels (many people we have relaxed say that they had quite forgotten what it felt like), you will be able to relax yourself quite quickly, whenever you need to. This is an important skill that is well worth much practice. (If you are unable to relax by yourself at the beginning, you may benefit from seeing a therapist who can do a guided relaxation with you. We often tape the relaxation part of therapy sessions, so clients can replay the tape and induce a relaxed state whenever they want to.)

Three ways to relax quickly

The following techniques are easy to learn. Although it may help the first time you try them for someone else to talk you through the steps (so you can focus on relaxing), this isn't essential as they are easy to remember. You can do them on your own whenever you need to.

1. The 7/11 method: Many people find that the easiest way to relax is to concentrate on their own breathing, so we suggest you try this method.

- Settle yourself comfortably somewhere that you won't be disturbed.

- Make sure your clothes are loose.

- Sit or lie comfortably with your hands side by side in your lap, or with your arms by your side, and your legs uncrossed.

- Close your eyes.

- Concentrate on becoming aware of your feet on the floor, of your legs and arms, wherever they are resting, and your head against the cushion, pillow or chair back.

- Begin to make each out-breath last longer than your in-breath. (This works because the out-breath stimulates the body's natural relaxation response. By changing your pattern of breathing in this way, your body automatically begins to relax.) A good way to do this is to breathe in to the count of 7, then breathe out gently and more slowly to the count of 11.

- Do this about 10 to 20 times, knowing that you will relax more each time. Concentrate on the counting (don't let your mind wander off) and feel the welcome sense of calm gradually flow in.

- Become aware of how much less tense you feel, just by relaxing your breathing and calming your thoughts, so you can recognise the feeling more easily in the future.

This 7/11 technique, as it is known, is good for instant

relaxation too. Just do it a few times, wherever you are, if you slip into thinking you can't cope without your addiction or feel so wound up that you can't make a simple decision, or are nervous, or want to burst into tears. (If you find it easier, substitute 3/5 for 7/11. The important thing is not the counting but that the out-breaths last longer than the in-breaths.)

2. The tight fist method: This second way to relax is derived from yoga. Settle yourself comfortably, then make your hands as tightly as possible into fists. (Only use this method if your hands and fingers are undamaged and move easily.)

- Look at your fists carefully as you scrunch them harder and harder, being aware of the whiteness of the knuckles, the feeling of your nails against your palms, the pressure of your thumbs against your forefingers, the rigidity of your wrists and notice the tension moving up your arms to your elbows and shoulders.

- Keep squeezing your fists like this and concentrate on the physical sensations for a minute or two.

- Then, to help you concentrate, close your eyes.

- Next, with all your concentration focused on your hands, allow your hands to slowly unwind and relax.

- Still with your eyes closed, feel the enjoyable sensation of relaxation spreading quite naturally through your fingers and up along your arms as the tension drains away. You may find it takes the form of whatever your body needs –

coolness if you tend to be too hot or warmth if you tend to feel too cold – or else you might just feel a pleasant tingling sensation.

- Whatever form it takes, let the relaxing sensation spread on through your body, smoothing your brow, your cheek muscles, your jaw, your shoulders, chest and so on, down to your toes.

- Keep your focus on the falling away of stress and the calming differences you can sense in your body.

- You can keep doing this as long as you like, simply enjoying noticing the calming changes that will occur throughout your body – and as your body relaxes so does your mind.

3. The whole body method: This method is also derived from yoga and achieves relaxation in a similar way.

- Work gradually through the main muscles of your body, tensing each in turn for a count of 10 and then relaxing them. As in the previous technique, this works on the simple mechanical principle that, if you tense muscles and then relax them, the muscles are always more relaxed than before you tensed them.

- You might start with your feet, move up to your calf muscles, then your knees, your thighs, your tummy muscles and so on.*

Create a 'special, peaceful place' in your mind

You can make relaxing an even more pleasant experience by using the time with your eyes closed to waft yourself away mentally to some pleasant imaginary place, or to a real place that you love to go to. People often choose to imagine walking on empty beaches by the sea, or in the mountains, or by a stream, or sitting in a beautiful garden. But you can make the scene whatever you want it to be, tranquil or lively.

If you relax more easily when there are other people around, incorporate their presence into your imaginings. Perhaps you relax through a sporting activity, such as playing football or squash, or cycling or swimming or walking in the hills, in which case visualise yourself enjoying that activity. Wherever you choose to be, and whatever you choose to do there, concentrate on making the occasion as real as it can be. If you are good at visualising things in your mind's eye, try to really *see* the colours of the flowers or the trees or the grass. *Hear* the sounds – the gentle whoosh of rippling waves, the rustling of leaves, the voices of people enjoying themselves. *Feel* the textures; *smell* the smells.

---

* A helpful relaxation CD, called *Relax: using your own innate resources to let go of pent-up stress and negative emotion*, is available from the publishers of this book. Tel: 01323 811662 or www.humangivens.com As well as relaxing you, using these techniques and others, the CD teaches you about the benefits of relaxation at the same time.

Imagine your chosen scene in detail, so that you can make it your very own 'special, safe place', somewhere you will always be able to call to mind and enjoy when relaxed – or to use to help you relax quickly when you need to be calm (such as before going into an interview or before having to deal with a difficult situation).

You need to remember to calm yourself down in one of these ways whenever addiction's illusions start to make you feel anxious, but *before* they overwhelm you. Just as you can't tense and relax a muscle at the same time, so you can't be anxiously aroused when you are in a relaxed state. When you are calm, you have access to the rational part of your brain and can more clearly recognise and question the illusory satisfactions addiction is offering.

Change your expectations

If you have indulged in your addictive activity for some time, you probably have thousands and thousands of memories and associations that urge you to 'go on and treat yourself' to it again. It is crucial that you are more than vigilant against these. You have to be ready at all times to counter those positive memories of, or thoughts about, the addictive activity with even more powerful negative ones. You need to be able to summon up embarrassing, guilt-inducing memories of times you have indulged, rather than rose-tinted unreal recollections of such occasions that will jump to the head of the queue.

This is enormously important. But you don't have to think of a million different negative associations, to counter all the different 'positive' ones in your memory bank. The same few compelling ones will do. In fact, the more you think of those compelling reasons not to indulge, and the nasty images they conjure up, the more embedded in your memory they will become.

> **❝ Never let a single positive thought about your addiction go unchallenged! ❞**

Never let a single positive thought about your addiction go unchallenged! But don't leave it there, or all you are doing is steeling yourself to do without something you wanted. Follow your counter-claim with a positive expectation that not having the addictive substance will actually be more fascinating, more productive, more enjoyable, or whatever. The end result is that you make a genuine *choice* not to indulge. And that means goodbye to unpleasant withdrawal symptoms. Here are some examples of what we mean.

Cuppa scupper

"I'd love another cup of coffee right now."
"When I have too many cups of coffee, my heart starts racing and I always hate that. It's frightening. I'm also likely to have a headache by the end of the day and that always brings me

down. There's nothing enjoyable about drinking coffee when all that is waiting for me."

"Mmm, but just remember that delicious coffee smell and that wonderful 'aaaah' feeling when you take the first sip. You feel all lovely and relaxed."

"Feeling relaxed only lasts for the first sip, and even that's an illusion. What I remember is feeling anxious and shaky if I don't have another coffee soon after. It was terrible that time I had three strong cups, one after another, while I was trying to meet my report deadline – my heart started banging so hard in my ribcage that I really thought I was going to have a heart attack. And anyway, coffee stops calcium being absorbed, so too much will give me brittle bones – and osteoporosis seems to run in my family."

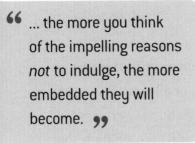

... the more you think of the impelling reasons *not* to indulge, the more embedded they will become.

"But there's nothing quite like a nice cup of coffee!"

"No, I'm sticking to my three – one at breakfast, one mid-morning and one in the evening. I'll really enjoy those three and will benefit by being headache-free all day. And I'm looking forward to trying out those new organic juice mixtures they are selling in the canteen. They taste lovely and are full of vitamins."

Smoking is a fag

"I'm going to die if I don't have a cigarette!"

"No, I'm not. I'm more likely to die if I *do* have a cigarette."

"Oh, but just smell the cigarette that girl over there is smoking! Doesn't she look contented!"

"Now that I too know what stale cigarette smoke is like on clothes, I know that it is revolting! I don't want to smoke! I don't want to have to worry about lung cancer and all those other cancers associated with smoking – like cancer of the mouth, oesophagus and tongue. And then there's heart disease and emphysema and bronchitis and having to have your legs amputated because of the effects on circulation. And it definitely makes your skin wrinkled and yellow-looking. I bet that girl over there wishes *she* could give up but she just doesn't know how to."

"But don't you remember the good old days and what it was like…?"

"Actually, it's great waking up in the morning without a sore throat. It's great being at work or in the cinema without dying to get out for a fag. I love the fact that my clothes and hair don't smell bad anymore. I love feeling powerful and in control. Everything I used to do with a fag in my hand I can still do just as well, and enjoy it just as much without. There's not one single way that smoking enhances my life."

Drink think

"It's been a helluva week. Wouldn't it be good to go to the pub again with the lads after work today, just this once?"

"I know that if I do that I'll get canned. It's this binge drinking I want to stop. Remember that terrifying article. It isn't just my liver that's at risk. Drinking heavily shrinks the brain and increases the risk of fits. It kills off brain cells, causing memory loss. Just three units of alcohol a day almost doubles my risk of cancer of the oesophagus, mouth and throat. It weakens muscles, joints and bones and, because the liver can't process it all, some gets excreted as sweat or in the breath, creating a strong, stale smell of alcohol. That's very fetching for attracting the opposite sex."

"But it's fun! Remember the time we all ended up in that club!"

"I remember getting blind drunk and someone else's sober girlfriend kindly giving me a lift on their way home and me being sick in the back of her car. I remember not being able to get my key in my door and having to wake up my elderly neighbour to let me in. I remember being absolutely mortified next day, after I'd stopped throwing up.

"Last Friday, I had a really good time when I went with my girlfriend round to some friends for dinner. We had a great laugh and got into some interesting discussions and I could really think out my ideas because I wasn't drinking. We all had a good time and I felt so energetic and well when I woke up the next morning."

Remind yourself of your resources

When you plan to let go of an addiction, you need to feel confident that you can do so. We don't mean by this that you should try to convince yourself that you are an incredible person who can do anything you set your hand to. We mean reminding yourself of all the resources genuinely at your disposal. Resources are based in reality. They are not hopes you have about yourself but actual skills you have already demonstrated, or practical support that is available to you, that you can turn to good use in meeting your goals.

Reminding yourself of your resources means reminding yourself not only of your talents and abilities but also of things you have successfully done in the past that can serve as resources to draw on in the future. A history of success in *any* area of your life is a resource, when dealing with addiction. Indeed, having tried to give up your addiction in the past, even if you succeeded only for a day or a week or for as long as a year, is a vital resource. Your experience will have given you information about what worked and what didn't and increases your chances of success this time round.

And reminding yourself of your resources is particularly important for building your confidence and showing you how you can meet unmet needs in healthy ways, rather than through addiction. If loneliness or boredom drives you to indulge in your problematic activity, it may be because you are missing out on close relationships or a social life. Perhaps, if your self-esteem is low, you think you are not competent enough to fill this need in your life. But, having had a long-term relationship of any kind tells you that

> " ... having tried to give up your addiction in the past is also a vital resource. "

you *are* capable of forming and maintaining relationships (even if addiction is trying to persuade you otherwise). Having had a caring relationship with anyone – for instance with your children, parents or as a professional carer – shows that you have the ability to connect with people, can put others first and can do so again. (By making us focus on immediate 'wants', addiction makes us selfish. Remembering previous instances of when you have cared for others proves that this hasn't always been the case and, therefore, need not be so in the future.)

If you have achieved educational or vocational qualifications, have passed a driving test or mastered skills such as playing the cello, knitting, typing or scuba diving, this shows you have the dedication and perseverance to achieve a goal and can therefore do so again. And don't forget such qualities as a sense of humour, the ability to persevere and kindness. All of these are important resources.

Make a list

List all the resources you can think of, however great or small, that will help you believe you can be successful. What are your personal strengths and your positive traits? Also list the resources available to you outside yourself – for instance, the support or goodwill of close family or friends, or having sufficient income to spend on taking a class, learning a new skill, entertaining at your home or whatever. Be as creative as you can be in your interpretation of what constitutes a resource! We will show you how to make even more use of them in the section "Visualise success!" (see page 148).

Separate yourself from the addiction

When you think about your reliance on your addictive activity and how uncomfortable, anxious and restless you may feel whenever you can't or don't perform it, do you think of yourself as addicted to that activity? Maybe you even think of yourself as 'an addict'. Alternatively, you may protest inside your head, "I am not an addict!" or "I am not addicted!" Either way, if you think about your addictive activity in any of these terms, you are identifying with the addiction, as if addiction could be part of your own personality instead of something entirely separate. It is as if you are in league with it, attached to it, part of it (this is so even if you are struggling to deny it). That in itself will make you feel hopeless and as if you have no control over it.

You will be taking a huge step forward in your journey out of addiction if you simply start to think of addiction as something alien to yourself. Just doing that small thing –

> **66** *You* are not the problem – the addiction is. **99**

using the noun 'addiction' (a noun being the name of a separate thing) instead of the adjective 'addicted' (an adjective describes something and is therefore a part of it) represents a powerful shift in your mindset!

Addiction instantly becomes something outside you, which you have been attracted and deceived by, but which you can equally well choose to wave away and have no further connection with.

When you see, *really* see, that you are not the addiction, you can start to alter your responses to it. In this frame of mind, you are accessing your 'observing self', the rational, analytical part of your brain, instead of the primitive (in the sense that it evolved first and we share it with animals) emotional brain we have described.

Try asking yourself the following questions. If you are not comfortable with the word 'addiction', substitute 'addictive activity'.

- What made you so vulnerable to addiction that it can now dominate your life?

- What are the circumstances that are usually going on when the addiction urges you to give in to it?

- What lies does the addiction tell you?

- What effect does the addiction have on your work/relationships?

- Does the addiction blind you from recognising your true strengths and resources?

- Are there times when you have been able to get the better of addiction?

- What was happening when addiction didn't get a look in?

Looking at addiction in this way should make it clear that *you* are not the problem: the addiction is. Instead of being a powerless partner, you are a strong, separate individual who can choose to turn your back on addiction.

Recognise unhelpful pattern matches

In Part 1 of this book, we introduced the *amygdala*, the structure in the brain that we dubbed the security officer. The amygdala has almost instant access to our innate survival instincts and our unconscious emotional memories and conditioned responses and acts on them. To recap, whenever we experience a sensation – a sound, a smell, a touch, a sight or a taste – the information is flashed in a nanosecond to the amygdala so that we can make sense of it by matching it to experiences that we have had in the past (a process we call pattern matching). In this way, we learn whether what is occurring is familiar or alien, safe or a possible threat.

By its very nature, this mechanism has to be relatively crude. If every time we see an apple, we have to treat it as an alien, possibly threatening object unless it has exactly the same colouring, shape and bruise patterns as apples we've seen before, we would be extremely hampered in our ability to get on with our lives. So, we see a roundish, reddish, greenish or yellowish object with a little stalk, within a certain size range and with a certain texture, and we register that it is an apple.

This works very well most of the time. But the process lets us down when we summon up associations from the past and assume that the outcome will be the same today. For instance, someone may wince and cower every time they see a person holding a hammer because they were once mugged by someone who threatened to hit them with one. Such mismatching has ramifications for addictive activity.

The story of Elise is typical of what can happen. She got extremely upset once when she had an argument with her husband that culminated in his storming out of the house. Left in a state of high emotional arousal with no apparent way to discharge it, Elise reached for the bottle. But the rows continued and the drinking gradually escalated until, after some time, she became aware that she was drinking more than she thought was good for her. So, all by herself, she successfully stopped drinking altogether. She no longer drank at social occasions or went for drinks with colleagues after work and felt justifiably proud of her achievement. Her relationship with her husband improved too. But one day she had another furious row with him. He slammed his way out of the house, making the windows shake, and Elise instantly pattern matched to the conditioned response of drowning her agitation in drink, thus setting herself up for a major relapse, because the sudden urge to drink felt so intense. This is exactly the type of situation in which the desire to drink (or indulge in whatever your particular addictive activity is) may become almost overwhelmingly powerful.

Breaking the connection

It is at these times that it is vital to remain alert and recognise the desire for what it is – an outdated association. As Elise had successfully managed not to drink on other occasions, she most probably realised that she did not need a drink on this one. However that realisation is very difficult to hold on to when emotions are overwhelming the rational mind. To get into her rational mind at times like this Elise needs to bring her emotional arousal down fast. She can handle it effectively in one of a number of ways. She might decide to go out herself, perhaps for a walk or a run. If that is not appropriate or possible, she could engage in an energetic indoor activity, such as cleaning or moving the furniture, which will serve to lower her arousal levels. She might choose instead to calm herself using one of the methods we described at the beginning of this section, or she might engage in a distracting activity, like phoning a sympathetic friend, listening to calming music or watching the television.

Other triggers

Another common trigger for an addictive activity is seeing someone else doing it – lighting up, having a cake, drinking steaming coffee, playing on a computer, taking a jog – or seeing an object that brings the addictive activity to mind. This is all because the amygdala has been carrying out its pattern matching and is triggering mild withdrawal symptoms. (Brain scans of cocaine addicts have shown that just seeing pictures of some of the paraphernalia associated with cocaine use activates the amygdala.)

Because the desire – which is an expectation – aroused by such associations is a deeply primitive thing, it is powerful and you need to be alert and ready to challenge it, whenever it arises. As we know, it is only by changing your memories and associations with the addictive activity that the pull of addiction fades. This remains important for a long time after you have stayed free of your addiction because sometimes, even years after stopping, you may have an experience that, for the first time since stopping, recalls the addictive activity to mind and reawakens desire.

One woman had successfully stopped smoking in September of one year and was amazed when she was hit with an almost overwhelming desire for a cigarette the day before going on holiday the following August. She quickly realised that it was the first time she had packed a suitcase since quitting smoking. The very act of deliberating about what to pack in the suitcase had summoned up the image of smoking. Having been a heavy smoker, smoking while packing was just another of the times when she had been accustomed to smoke. Fortunately, she was able to stand back, look dispassionately at the impulse to smoke, see where it had come from, and reject it by reminding herself of all the negatives of smoking and the positives of not smoking.

Buy yourself time

Addictive impulses can appear to be more powerful than they really are. So much so that, when they occur, you may rush to satisfy the impulse, or to start making plans to satisfy it, before you quite realise what you are doing. One useful way to hoodwink addiction in such circumstances is to buy yourself time. Tell yourself, "I won't do it just now/ I won't start planning it now; I'll give it 15 minutes and perhaps start then." Doing that gives you a chance to get out of your emotional brain, with its childish demands and sulks, and back into your rational mind, which you can use to make a calm, considered choice to reject the impulse.

Traumatic memories

IF YOU are pattern matching to a traumatic experience that still intrudes into your life, perhaps in the form of panic attacks, flashbacks or nightmares, you should see a therapist who can help you take the emotional power out of the memories, so that they cease to cause these symptoms. All human givens therapists are trained to do this. We describe the method on pages 198–9. ●

Visualise success!

Using your imaginative skills is a highly effective means of breaking an unhelpful, inappropriate pattern match and replacing it with a better one. Your imagination is one of the most powerful resources you have. It is as powerful as our thoughts – or even more powerful, as it engages strong emotions. Thus you can use it to make your withdrawal from addiction as painful and frustrating as it could possibly be (which is probably what you have done, unwittingly, up till now); *or* you can use your imagination to overcome addiction positively and painlessly.

Our imagination enables us to generate different possible realities, solve problems and rehearse success, giving us the ability to create and 'view', in the 'theatre' of our mind, scenarios other than the one we are currently in. It is the evolution of this 'reality generator', the ability to imaginatively daydream, that marks us out from animals. But it is a powerful tool and, like all powerful tools, can be used for good or ill. So, we can bring to mind our dopamine-soaked inaccurate *attractive* memories of indulging in our addiction and use them to drive ourselves mad with desire to cheat ourselves yet again. Or we can use it to bring different images to mind that make the addictive activity seem highly *unattractive* and to create scenarios in which we successfully try out different responses and experience better outcomes. The choice is ours.

How to harness the power of expectation

When you visualise a future event for yourself, you are harnessing the power of expectation. (You see this power in action with people who think of themselves as lucky – they tend to be lucky, whereas people who think of themselves as unlucky tend to be unlucky. They act in ways that support their expectation, and maximise the likelihood of the expected outcome.) For people who have an addiction, expecting either to be unable to survive or else to be miserable without it maximises the chances of relapse.

Therefore we strongly advise you to use the power of expectation for yourself in ways that will help you reject your addiction. This is not an 'airy-fairy' notion. It is a concrete, learnable skill. Take a time when you can be uninterrupted for at least 15 minutes or so, and relax, using one of the methods we suggested previously if you need to.

Visualise the <u>negatives</u> of addiction

When you are relaxed, think about your problematic activity. Bring vividly to mind all the scenarios associated with it that make you feel disgusted and guilty about indulging in it and frightened about its harmful effects on your life.

If, for example, your problem is bulimia – you overeat and purge – think of how greedy you feel when you start to binge; how you have no enjoyment in the food you stuff into your mouth; how bloated and disgusted you soon feel; how disgusted you are when you make yourself sick; see your teeth rotting in your mouth from the acid in your vomit, smell your foul bulimic breath, remember how embarrassed you have been on any occasion when someone realised or suspected what you were doing; recall how bad you felt about yourself afterwards and how you felt just as upset and lonely as before you started. Recall any specific times when something really bad happened because of your indulgence in your addiction. Visualise your worst fears becoming fact – developing diabetes, having a heart attack or experiencing other serious internal damage. Imagine being left by your partner, because he or she is disgusted with you. Imagine dying of avoidable illness, thus being unable to bring up your children and see them progress through their lives.

If your addiction is smoking, drug-taking or drinking to excess, bring vividly to mind every article you have ever shuddered at, that describes all the physical damage that these activities do. Don't spare yourself from the horror of it. Imagine what it would be like to have lung cancer so you can barely breathe, or cancer of the mouth or throat rotting your face away, or to suffer a massive heart attack or need a liver transplant. See the faces of those who loved you in agonies of distress as you die at a younger age than you should.

> **66 Your imagination is one of the most powerful resources you have. 99**

If your addiction takes the form of an activity rather than a substance, evoke as realistically as possible the guilt you feel after spending hours, say, online at the computer, instead of being with your family, or the let-down and guilt you feel when you arrive home with another expensive consumer item you can't afford and consign it to a cupboard. Picture the disappointment or horror on the faces of those you love. Conjure up a scenario in which, because of the huge amount of money you are wasting, your home is at risk or your loved ones have to suffer. Come up with your worst possible fears, the worse-case scenarios, (perhaps you are stealing to fund your habit – what if you went to prison?) and live them out in your imagination – even if they are exaggerated. If you have been calling up false memories to support you in continuing your habit, you can just as effectively embed exaggerated memories to help you beat it.

Visualise the <u>positives</u> of being free of addiction

Now, if you have disgusted and frightened yourself half to death, it is important that you calm yourself down again before you start to bring to mind all the good things you will experience when you are not indulging in your addictive activity. Perhaps you feel physically better (be specific as to how). You look so much better, because you are living more healthily. You have time to spend on activities you ceased to have time for before – whether old pleasures or new ones. Perhaps you have significantly more money and can spend it on things that will enhance your own and your family's lives. Your friends and family are so much happier. You have bags of energy and you sleep better. You love feeling in control of your life, instead of constantly worrying about, and succumbing to, your ultimately always unsatisfying addiction.

Again, fill in the concrete details so that you are really seeing yourself in these new situations, experiencing these positive outcomes and any others that you think of. Bask in the delight of feeling free!

Repeat often

Empower yourself in this way with your own imagination as often as you find helpful. (This is very different from positive thinking, which is often just wishful thinking and not rooted in reality at all. Strong emotions, such as anxiety, depression, anger, disgust, lust and greed, always override thought. It is by engaging emotions in this powerful way that we change the way the brain pattern matches to previous experiences. This is one of the main reasons why the human givens approach is so effective.) Visualising the terrible and the terrific will create strong, new patterns for your brain to match to when you experience an urge to perform your compulsive activity, and help relegate withdrawal symptoms to just a pathetic little rumble or twinge.

Use these images to help you challenge any single positive image of addiction that sneaks into mind – remember, you probably have thousands of them. Do not let a single one pass unchallenged or you risk allowing addiction to regain a foothold on your life.

> 66 By engaging our emotions in this powerful way we change the way the brain pattern matches to previous experiences. 99

Depending upon how entrenched your reliance on your addiction has been, it might take up to a year before positive addictive images totally stop coming to mind at all, and you reject any such impulses automatically, before they even reach consciousness. In the meantime, momentarily calling to mind both the negatives of the addiction and the positives of not giving in to it is a small price to pay for a pain-free passage out of addiction.

Develop strategies to use in high-risk situations

Making plans for how you will deal with those situations in which you are likely to be tempted is crucial for your success. We would even go so far as to say that, if you just 'hope' you won't succumb to your old addiction if you find yourself in such a tempting setting, you have already decided to re-engage in your addictive activity. *But, if you plan in advance what you will do and how you will respond in that situation, you are already in control of the addictive process.* The first important thing is to be sure you know your triggers.

What triggers a strong addictive impulse for you?

Take a moment to consider the list of potential triggers below and make a note of your answers.

- Being with particular people? If so, who?
- Being in particular places? If so, where?
- Doing particular activities? If so, what?
- When experiencing extremely negative feelings (for instance, feeling worthless, upset, angry, lonely, bored, depressed)?
- When experiencing extremely positive feelings (for instance, excitement or elation)?
- When experiencing sensations that recall the addictive activity? If so, what are they?

If you recognise that you have strong urges when you are with particular people or in a particular place, you do not need to avoid those people or that place *unless* their sole connection is with addiction. (By that we mean people who share your addiction but no other part of your life, or a place you go to only to indulge your addiction.) But you do need to take steps to minimise any temptation, if you put yourself in the way of it.

Suppose you are stopping smoking. As well as being ready to summon your negative and positive expectations, which will reinforce your decision not to have a cigarette, you might decide that, the first time you go to a pub with smokers, you will ensure that some non-smokers are also in the party, so that you aren't the only one refusing a cigarette. Alternatively you might decide, initially, that you need to remove yourself from the tempting situation occasionally – perhaps by taking a walk round the block or going to make a phone call – to give yourself time to challenge your expectations and experience them emotionally.

It's also a good idea to have a reason ready, just in case others who also indulge in your addictive activity ask why you aren't joining in anymore. If it doesn't feel appropriate to launch into explaining what an illusion the 'pleasure' from addiction is, you could always say something like, "I'm just having a break" or "I've got a sore throat/sore head".

If you know that you give in to your addictive activity when you're alone and bored, make sure that you always have a diverting activity available that you enjoy. It could be doing a bit of gardening, completing a crossword or jigsaw, having a friend willing to be called for support, reading a gripping book, cleaning out a cupboard or starting to refurbish a room. It is no good just telling yourself life will be wonderful without your addiction if you haven't thought about instant ways to satisfy your needs in a healthy way when a low mood catches you unawares.

Expect setbacks in life

Life is transient, full of the unexpected. We learn with a shock, for instance, that the firm we have worked at for 30 years is to close. A loved one is badly injured in a car crash. A marriage ends. A life partner dies. We are passed over for promotion. Our possessions are destroyed in a fire. A baby is stillborn.

Wise people know they do not need addiction to help them cope with loss and tragedy – countless people before have survived great difficulties without succumbing, and addiction doesn't, in reality, even mask the pain. We all have to endure shocks and grieve from time to time … and then do what we can to move on. It's part of life.

So be prepared for change. Nothing is constant. Even the stars die. Whenever you are brought up short by an unexpected setback, whatever your degree of loss, be ruthless with yourself. Ask, "In what way will it help me and those around me if I take up addiction again?" The accurate answer is always, "In no way at all".

Enjoy a healthier lifestyle

Whatever the emotional needs you have identified as not being met sufficiently well in your life, don't forget the needs of your body. We all need a good diet and regular exercise to stay healthy. Even if your addictive activity has been over-exercise, or over- or under-eating, you need to find a healthy middle way.

A good diet does much to undo the damage of addiction and lessen the likelihood of relapse. Addiction to stimulants such as coffee, tea, sugar, carbonated drinks, chocolates, cigarettes and certain drugs plays havoc with the well-being of your body, causing depletion of important vitamins and minerals and a general imbalance that adversely affects health. Junk food, which is designed purposefully to become addictive, harmfully affects the moods and physical health of children and adults. Alcoholism causes significant nutritional deficiency, as of course does anorexia. People who smoke cigarettes often do so to keep appetite at bay, so that they eat less. Workaholics and those who indulge in time-intense addictions, such as gambling and computer game-playing, often forget to eat properly.

You can also help your body recover from the ravages of addiction by ensuring you have a healthy diet, including plenty of fresh fruit and vegetables, wholegrain cereals, breads, pasta and other wholefoods such as lentils, beans, nuts, seeds, eggs, cold-pressed seed oils; and fish such as herring, mackerel, salmon or fresh tuna. (Instead of eating fish regularly, you may prefer to take an omega-3 fish oil supplement, as pollution in the sea is an increasing problem. Two grams is a good preventive or maintenance dose and is equal to two teaspoons of cod liver oil, which can be bought quite cheaply in bottles.) And drink plenty of ordinary water.

> **"** Different addictive substances deplete the body of different nutrients ... **"**

Different addictive substances deplete the body of different nutrients in varying amounts. For a nutritional approach that is tailored to help the body recover from specific addictions and to find a clinical nutritionist trained in this approach, visit mentalhealthproject.com

Exercise keeps you in shape and lifts the mood (by raising serotonin levels). The physical benefits to your body and the good feelings that ensue will also help you live rewardingly without addiction. Make sure that whatever exercise you take is enjoyable and perhaps brings you into contact with other people. The exercise will then become another means of focusing attention away from yourself and your preoccupation with addiction, and of spending enjoyable time with others.

Deal positively with relapse

As we have seen, relapse is almost an integral part of stopping an addictive activity so don't berate yourself unduly if it happens to you. Research on smokers, heroin addicts and alcoholics who have tried to give up the habit shows that about two-thirds relapse within three months, most within the first month. Four out of five people who try to give up an addiction don't manage it at the first attempt. Research on smoking has shown that it usually takes three or four serious attempts to give up before final, lasting success is achieved.

> 66 Relapse is almost an integral part of stopping an addiction, so don't berate yourself unduly if it happens to you. 99

If you do find yourself taking that cigarette and lighting it, downing that bottle of wine, having a joint, paying a visit to the betting shop, picking up a stranger in a bar or having four cups of coffee before breakfast on a particularly frazzled morning, try not to brand yourself a hopeless failure. Instead, mentally make the relapse a little wobble in your learning curve and use the following positive ways to help you deal with it.

Stop

Remove yourself from the relapse situation, if there is still time, and go somewhere quiet where you can think about what has happened.

Stay calm

Don't let yourself panic, even if you feel scared or shocked by what you have done. You need your observing self to be in charge at this point, so that you can check out what triggered you to succumb to addiction. Push away guilt and blame and concentrate instead on how to move forwards.

Find the explanation

There is probably a clear, easily identifiable reason why you relapsed.

- Did you experience a strong negative or positive emotion that you usually push away or try to enhance by means of the addictive activity?

- Have you experienced a setback in your life, minor or severe, that undermined your resolve?

- Did you experience a sensation or event that strongly called up the memory of a past occasion when you indulged the addiction, and which resulted in an over-whelming craving?

- Did addiction trick you into thinking you could safely test yourself now, just to prove that you are no longer addicted?

Whatever your answer, this is important information. It tells you when you need to be extra-vigilant and that you cannot yet let your guard fall.

Review your commitment

Instead of going into all-or-nothing emotional thinking ("I had one cigarette/biscuit/drink, so I might as well have 20"; "Addiction has beaten me again. It is stronger than I am and I'll never beat it"), this is the time to affirm to yourself that you choose not to be enslaved by addiction. You have had a warning that you still need to work at challenging positive expectations of addiction. So remind yourself of how successfully you have managed to do this so far. Remind yourself, too, that addiction is a formidable adversary but that your powerful inner resources enable you to be the stronger one, if you let them work *for* you.

Plan for what you do next

View your lapse as a temporary departure from your 'roadmap' and decide to get back on track. What do the circumstances of the lapse tell you? Are any of your important needs unmet at the moment? If so, how can you take effective action to work towards meeting them?

Ask for help

Turn for support to friends and family who have your best interests at heart. (Avoid any who might welcome your lapse, for whatever reason.) Seeking help will also reassure those who had faith in you that you still mean to stick with your resolve. You might also consider seeing an effective therapist, if you feel you could benefit from outside help in strengthening your resolve.

In the final part of this book, we will show you how effective therapy can help.

QUICK CHECK – your plan for beating addiction

Our addiction knows us inside out. It knows all our vulnerable points. So, if we are going to defeat it, we have to know how to outwit it. Every successful addiction plan has the following three key elements:

1 Knock out the positive expectations that addiction feeds you

By constantly bringing into our consciousness all of our worst, most painful, embarrassing memories connected with the addictive behaviour, we can counter the positive expectations that addiction brings to the fore. It is then important to strengthen our motivation with positive, wonderful images of being free from addiction – in control of our life again, free from guilt, financially secure, with a new or renewed sense of autonomy and volition, with restored feelings of self-worth and plenty of energy.

2 Revamp your lifestyle to get your needs met more successfully

Use your needs audit to help you see where important needs are not being met in your life and start taking the necessary steps to remedy this. Remember, when you are fulfilled in your life, you do not need addiction.

3 Anticipate high-risk situations

A high-risk situation can be any person, place or thing that you connect habitually to the addictive behaviour. So meeting an old friend with whom you used to do cocaine, heroin, gamble or get drunk, for example, may, through pattern matching, trigger off a desire to carry out the addictive behaviour again. You may be surprised at how strong that desire can be, even if you haven't indulged in the addictive behaviour for some time.

The trick is to prepare for situations that you know are high risk and work out a strategy to knock out temptation *before* it hits.

Keep uppermost in your mind the fact that your addiction lies to you. It continually makes false promises that it doesn't fulfil. It always creates more pain and more problems in real life than it appears to solve.

And also remember that a favourite strategy of addiction is getting you emotionally worked up so that you can't see the bigger picture clearly. When we get emotional (go into a state of 'wanting'), the intelligent part of our brain (the 'boss') gets switched off and we can't see through the lies the addiction is telling us. A good way not to fall for that one is to buy yourself time. Decide not to make any decision for 15 minutes and during that time allow yourself to calm down. Then you will be able to remember clearly why you want to beat the addiction, and the desire will most probably melt away. The intensity of the desire is only momentary, if you don't give it house room.

In advance, prepare a list of healthy non-addictive alternatives to the compulsive activity – such as going for a brief walk, phoning a supportive friend, drinking a glass of water, eating a piece of fruit, doing a relaxation technique, introducing a new topic of conversation, leaving early, etc.

If we knowingly go into a high-risk situation without a coping strategy/plan in our minds, we are inviting the addiction back into our life.

PART 3

Seeking professional help

A LOT of people will find that the insights and guidance in the first parts of this book are enough to help them tackle their addiction straight away, and with great success. On the other hand, perhaps, like many others, you want some extra help to get started on the road out of addiction and decide to seek the aid of a psychotherapist or counsellor (the two words mean the same, so we will use the word 'therapist' to cover them both). If you take this route, there are three important things that you need to be aware of.

1. It is no good expecting a therapist to cure you

You have to want to cure yourself. Effective therapists can build on your motivation and help you learn the skills that others have used successfully to beat addictions. They can also help you learn the skills or recognise the steps you need to take to meet your unmet needs in a healthier way. But they absolutely cannot get rid of your addiction for you.

2. You can't indulge in 'magical thinking'

Dealing with addiction takes commitment and perseverance on your part. If you have chosen to quit rather than cut down on your addictive activity, it is inappropriate to test whether the therapy has 'worked' by indulging in the addictive activity again. *You* must do the work, not the therapy.

3. Finding an effective therapist is not straightforward

Incredible as it may seem, there are over 400 different schools of therapy, all with their own ideas of how different psychological difficulties should be treated. Imagine if there were that many ways to treat a physical illness! So you really need to be confident that your therapist's approach is appropriate for helping you overcome addictive behaviour as quickly and effectively as possible.

Unfortunately, most schools of therapy follow a particular 'model' of therapy, which they may apply to the exclusion of all others. Behaviour therapists, for example, will concentrate on setting tasks designed to help you beat your addiction. Cognitive therapists are more interested in helping you change the way you think about things, as a means of helping you overcome your addictive behaviour. Cognitive-behavioural therapy is a mixture of the two, and is the treatment usually offered by clinical psychologists. (However, it is a rather long, drawn-out business.) Person-centred therapists (most counsellors in GP surgeries are of this type) believe that the solution lies hidden somewhere inside you and that, if they keep listening to you talk, with a few prods in particular directions, you will find the way for yourself. Psychodynamic therapists believe that, before you can overcome addiction, you have to dig up past pains and insecurities and major disappointments to understand why you became addicted in the first place.

Many of these different schools of therapy have got hold of a part of the truth but unfortunately they stick to that one part and hone it, to the exclusion of everything else. This tends to unbalance the work of therapists, however well-meaning, who work from within such limited models. Of course, it is good to set people tasks to help them change problem behaviours or to help people become aware of and question negative thinking, or to listen to people with empathy, *but none of these approaches is sufficient on its own.*

All the major organisations that accredit or register psychotherapists and counsellors include on their registers practitioners who specialise in these less-than-effective therapies. So how people term themselves professionally, which organisations or trade associations they belong to or are accredited by, and how much training they have had, are not reliable guides as to how effective they are in helping people. This makes it very difficult for vulnerable people seeking professional help and for GPs wishing to refer patients to someone with psychological expertise in dealing with emotional problems.

The human givens approach to psychotherapy and counselling, which we teach at Human Givens College, offers a way out of this dilemma.* We have stripped out the ideological beliefs and the cult-like preciousness of so much counselling practice. The main focus is on enabling people to get their needs met and make full and effective use of their innate resources. This means we apply whatever mixture of tried and tested techniques will help best to do that, making judgements according to individual circumstances.

66 The main focus of human givens therapy is to help people get their needs met. 99

* To find a human givens therapist close to your area, call Human Givens College on +44 (0)1323 811690 or visit: www.hgi.org.uk/register/

Checklist for finding an effective therapist

We stress that an effective psychotherapist or counsellor will:

- understand depression and how to lift it (depression commonly accompanies addiction)

- understand the processes involved in addiction and how to overcome them

- help immediately with anxiety problems including trauma (post-traumatic stress disorder) or other fear-related symptoms

- be prepared to give advice if needed or asked for

- not use jargon or 'psychobabble'

- not dwell unduly on the past

- be supportive when difficult feelings emerge, but not encourage people to remain in an emotionally aroused state

- assist individuals in developing social skills, so that their needs for affection, friendship, pleasure, intimacy, connection to the wider community, etc. can be better fulfilled

- help people to draw on their own resources (which may prove greater than thought)

- be considerate of the effects of counselling on the people close to the individual concerned

- induce and teach deep relaxation

- help people think about their problems in a new and more empowering way

- use a wide range of techniques

- set tasks to be done between sessions

- take as few sessions as possible

- increase self-confidence and independence and make sure clients feel better after every consultation.

This list and the information in this book should be your guide to finding an effective therapist or counsellor. Therapists who work in tune with the human givens (even if they are not familiar with the term itself) will be happy with this list and understand it.

Spare capacity

Whatever type of therapist you see, you need to be sure that they have the 'spare capacity' to work with you. Someone who is preoccupied with their own personal concerns or troubles will not be able to distance themselves sufficiently to work with yours. Clearly, this has to be a matter of judgement on your part but there is much to be gleaned from an individual's manner – are they relaxed, warm and comfortable to be with or are they slightly anxious, brittle, fail to give you their full attention and too keen to push you to talk about (or not talk about) issues that reflect their own unresolved concerns? The therapist's responsibility is to work to help *you*. You should not feel that you need to help the therapist.

Shared experience is not important ...

Some people think that their therapist needs to be someone who has conquered the same addiction or has had a similar set of life experiences – otherwise how can they possibly understand and be helpful? But this is quite irrelevant in the human givens approach. Because the emphasis is on what clients can do to meet their *own* needs, human givens therapists can work with anyone. It doesn't make any difference what age you are, what ethnic background you come from, what religion you do or don't follow, or what sexual orientation you have. You establish, with the therapist's help, what needs are not being met in *your* life and set your own goals. The reality or world they are concerned with is yours, not theirs.

... but imaginative therapy *is* important

We have already described the huge importance of being able to relax and to use your imagination to help you overcome addiction. This is just as important a tool in human givens therapy – all human givens therapists have the ability to relax clients deeply, making use of that relaxed state to introduce positive suggestions and ideas to encourage resolve, and to help people use their imaginations to rehearse success.

When you are relaxed, the right (visual, more intuitive) hemisphere of your brain is dominant, while the left hemisphere (which is more involved in language, analysis and rational thought) takes a break. It is the right hemisphere that is most directly connected with our instinctive responses and is active when we dream, and its natural way of working is through metaphor. We are using metaphor whenever we describe something in terms of something else or say that something is like something else – for instance, nectarines are smooth peaches or the blackened sky is like an angry scowl. Metaphors conjure up imagery that we can instantly relate to, and which resonate with our more open and imaginative right hemisphere of the brain. Thus, by bypassing the often resistant or negative rational part of our brain, we can take on board new ideas and useful analogies.

For this reason, metaphor is powerful, and is used a great deal in the human givens approach, to create images that will have particular resonance for the person hearing them. For instance, talking of creating a 'balance sheet' to weigh up the pros and cons of addiction may have especial meaning for an accountant. And a wonderful way to use metaphor is in the form of story – for example the tale of how the Greek hero Odysseus, whilst sailing home from war, chose to resist the false song of the Sirens and thus avoided being shipwrecked on the shore is often told to people wanting to overcome addictions. Each takes from it something of personal meaning to them – and not necessarily all the same thing. (There is no one-size-fits-all approach in this kind of therapy.) Our natural pattern-matching facility leads us to make an unconscious link between the metaphor or story and our own life, and take on board what is useful to us.

Human givens therapy: how it has helped others with addiction

As we have seen, the human givens approach takes account of the full range of human nature and human needs. Therapists working on addiction listen with empathy and encourage their clients to weigh up for themselves the perceived benefits and risks of the addictive activity and to see the discrepancy between how they are living now and the goals they want to reach. They make a point of acknowledging their clients' past successes and personal resources, thus motivating them to realise that they *can* change, if they choose to. They help people to identify which of their unmet needs they are trying to fulfil through addiction, and to recognise and choose other healthier, more satisfying ways to meet those needs, making full use of their own innate resources to do so. Human givens therapists then apply whatever mixture of tried and tested techniques will help best to do that, making judgements according to individual circumstances.

In the pages that follow, we open our casebooks to show

you how the human givens approach can help people with addiction.

By now it will be clear that, to help yourself overcome your addictive behaviour, you need to bring to mind as many negative associations with the activity as you can. And, as we have seen, the more you remind yourself of these negative consequences, the more easily they will come to the fore when you feel a strong desire, however momentary, to indulge in the addiction. So, to help you focus on the negative effects and associations related to your addiction, we will also take a detailed look (in the boxes alongside each case), at what is known about the possible, probable or inevitable effects of each addiction on health and wellbeing. This should help you with imagining unpleasant scenarios that you can use in your own visualisations, as you work to reject addiction.

Tanya and her hippo's camp

Seventeen-year-old Tanya suffers from an extremely rare blood disorder (Golden Har Syndrome) and also from one of its side effects, scoliosis – a problem with the backbone causing curvature of the spine. When she was only 14, she was told that she was not expected to live beyond 16 – an obviously terrifying prospect for a child to deal with. Desperate to have fun and live life to the full while she still could, she ran away from home to live with her boyfriend.

But her mum made her return and shortly afterwards Tanya became depressed and stopped eating. She learned to ignore the hunger sensations when she was hungry and soon ceased to have any appetite at all.

Continually worried that her time was limited and convinced that her health would deteriorate dramatically when she reached 16, she spent the next year and a half doing whatever she wanted to do. Throughout this time she continued to have trouble eating and in fact hadn't eaten at all for two days when, a week before her 17th birthday, she was admitted to hospital with extremely severe vomiting. She ended up in intensive care, in a coma for five days. Her failure to eat and drink had caused a kidney disorder and exacerbated her blood disorder.

When she finally recovered, she felt she had achieved a "double survival". Not only had she cheated death at 16 but now she had also survived a real near-death experience at 17. Yet six months later, she was again depressed and started to cut out food once more, not caring about the consequences. Her mother, desperate to get Tanya interested in something, persuaded her to enrol in an animation course at a training centre for young people. It was here that Tanya met Pamela Woodford, a human givens therapist who works at the centre. Because she was worried about her attitude to eating, Tanya decided to see Pamela.

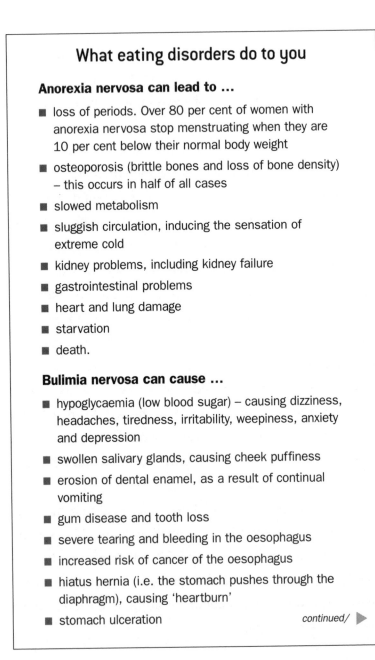

What eating disorders do to you

Anorexia nervosa can lead to ...

- loss of periods. Over 80 per cent of women with anorexia nervosa stop menstruating when they are 10 per cent below their normal body weight
- osteoporosis (brittle bones and loss of bone density) – this occurs in half of all cases
- slowed metabolism
- sluggish circulation, inducing the sensation of extreme cold
- kidney problems, including kidney failure
- gastrointestinal problems
- heart and lung damage
- starvation
- death.

Bulimia nervosa can cause ...

- hypoglycaemia (low blood sugar) – causing dizziness, headaches, tiredness, irritability, weepiness, anxiety and depression
- swollen salivary glands, causing cheek puffiness
- erosion of dental enamel, as a result of continual vomiting
- gum disease and tooth loss
- severe tearing and bleeding in the oesophagus
- increased risk of cancer of the oesophagus
- hiatus hernia (i.e. the stomach pushes through the diaphragm), causing 'heartburn'
- stomach ulceration

continued/ ▶

At their first meeting, she told Pamela that, although she didn't like her eating behaviour, what she really cared most about was hurting her family – she knew her mother was extremely worried about her. She also said that, as it was now nearly a year since she had been hospitalised due to the kidney disorder, she was expecting it to happen again at any moment. Pamela could see that Tanya was pattern matching to her past illnesses and to what she thought was 'expected' of her. As Tanya put it, "I've been ill all my life, so it didn't bother me, really, if I was ill again." After chatting with Pamela, who described the process of pattern matching, she realised that being ill was an expectation, "along with the anorexia, popping up its ugly head". And that she had also become addicted to her strange eating behaviour.

Making use of Tanya's keen interest in animation, Pamela suggested they drew pictures of the brain, while she explain-

---

Bulimia continued/

- muscle weakness and numbness (caused by potassium deficiency)
- swollen ankles and fingers
- breast tenderness
- congestive heart failure
- colon damage, caused by chronic laxative abuse
- feelings of self-loathing.

ed the expectation theory of addiction in detail. They drew the hippocampus (the part of the brain that stores our memories) as a 'hippo's camp' and the amygdala (the security officer, as we described it earlier) as 'Amy's data' – in other words, a diary. Tanya could picture these clearly, and herself as the 'boss'.

"At that life-changing moment, I realised my mind was playing games with me," she told Pamela later. "Understanding what was going on in my head was weird, extraordinary, and it has changed the way I think. 'Writing things' in my 'diary' and putting new memories and associations in the hippo's camp makes me laugh. I now have different hippocampus files that say I need food to live and to move and have fun and to stop my mum from nagging".

> 66 At that life-changing moment, I realised my mind was playing games with me ... 99

Tanya had four sessions with Pamela and since then has been eating good nutritious food (Pamela suggested she ate sardines for the omega-3 oils, so she had added those as 'good foods' to her hippo's camp). She is now actively trying to put on weight and had understood the expectation theory so well that she was able to use it to help her boyfriend cut down his cannabis use.

She has finished her animation course, and is now studying art and photography, with the hope either of getting a job or going on to art college. Pamela saw her again recently and is pleased to report that Tanya is thriving. "She's very happy and living the full life of any 18-year-old. Her expectations now are to live and to marry."

Leslie's drink problem

Leslie was a 32-year-old psychiatric nurse from the Midlands. He had fallen into the habit of going to the pub after work, to relax after the stresses of his job and to avoid going home to his miserable wife (she was suffering from depression, partly as a result of his behaviour). When he did finally go home, drunk, there would inevitably be arguments. As a result, his wife would become more depressed and Leslie more desperate. His sleep was soon affected too, leaving him tired at work the next day and thus even less able to cope, and so the cycle perpetuated itself.

Having decided that the situation had gone on for long enough, Leslie went to see Ivan for help. During their discussion, Ivan explained the mechanics of addictive drinking and the pattern matching process. He also encouraged Leslie to think about his worst fears, should he continue his current behaviour. Understandably, Leslie was highly anxious about losing his job and the possibility of ending up on the street, if his wife threw him out. (This had happened to a former colleague of his, who had developed a similar drink problem.) So next Ivan relaxed him and made use of guided imagery to help Leslie actually 'see' himself in his worst scenario, to picture himself in detail – perhaps lying slumped in the street, in a pool of his own vomit, after a hard night's drinking. His superior at the hospital, passing in his car, sees him there, reports him and he receives the dreaded warning. But he carries on drinking nonetheless and loses his job. Eventually, with no friends or family to help him, he finds himself dependent for company on other hardened, homeless drinkers, and they sit on street corners together, knocking back meths, being pointedly ignored or pitied by passers by.

Ivan then took the time to remind Leslie of his many resources and skills. For instance, he reminded him that he did have the ability to maintain a successful relationship, as his marriage had been good once, and pointed out what a caring and efficient nurse Leslie had been before he became stressed and turned to drink. Ivan then encouraged Leslie to visualise himself, full of energy again, putting his heart into his job, and enjoying a calmer home life.

On reflection, Leslie decided that he had no interest in cutting down on drink. Sitting in a pub nursing half a pint of beer all evening was not for him; he preferred the idea of giving up drinking entirely for two months, to see if he felt any better. He also agreed to go to the gym for an hour a few nights a week, both to improve his fitness and to fill his former after-work drinking time more healthily. Whenever he was tempted to go to the pub, he would bring to mind his

What alcohol does to you

Long-term drinking to excess (more than 21 units of alcohol a week for women and 28 for men – one unit being a half pint of beer, a small glass of wine or a pub measure of spirits) can lead to ...

- memory loss and confusion – alcohol is the third highest cause of dementia
- shrinkage of the brain that can increase the risk of epileptic fits
- inflammation and cirrhosis of the liver – irreparable scarring and impaired function
- high blood pressure
- heart attacks
- stroke
- cancer of the mouth, throat and pharynx
- cancer of the oesophagus
- cancer of the breast – drinking five units a day increases the risk by over 40 per cent
- muscle degeneration
- impaired eyesight and even blindness
- the skin conditions rosacea (reddened facial skin) and psoriasis, as well as increased wrinkling
- reduced fertility
- pancreatitis – inflammation of the pancreas that causes abdominal pain
- osteoporosis
- gout
- stomach ulcers.

worst-case scenario and all the other negatives associated with drinking (see: "What alcohol does to you" on page 181).

Leslie saw Ivan three more times in the next three months.

> **❝ Very quickly, he reported, his sleep had improved and he had more energy ... ❞**

Very quickly, he reported, his sleep had improved, so he felt more full of energy. And, as he was home, sober, at a reasonable hour every evening, the confrontations with his wife came to an end and they started to be able to have sensible conversations again. This helped his wife's depression to lift and they subsequently realised, while talking calmly, that neither of them had actually been happy in the relationship for some years and so, as they had no children, they agreed amicably to separate.

Having got back control of his life, and resolved matters with his wife, Leslie decided his life was significantly better when he was off the drink. He was soon finding his work rewarding once more and eventually started dating again. He had just one relapse in three years.

The workaholic

Alex, 38, had been a successful businessman. On the strength of his success, he had expanded his freight transport business, borrowing heavily to buy more lorries. But, as a result of other unforeseen costs, such as a sharp rise in the price of diesel, profits had started to plummet and he was working every hour he could just to try to pay back his loans. As a result, he spent less and less time at home. His wife Jane, who spent her days caring for their two young children, found she was spending most evenings alone and, lacking adult company, quite quickly sank into depression. Alex then became depressed too. It was only when he managed to get himself out of his depression that he realised his real problem was his addiction to work. He ran his business on rigid lines and, despite having an able staff, took most of the responsibilities on to himself.

Alex went to see Joe for help when Jane was on the point of breaking up their marriage, convinced that he would never change his ways. Joe helped Alex to think more objectively about his life, and Alex soon realised that he derived his 'buzz' in life almost entirely from work. His own father had been a workaholic who valued little other than hard work and so Alex had seen becoming a workaholic himself as the only way to gain his father's approval. On the other hand, he loved his wife and children dearly and recognised that he was missing out on his children's development. He realised he did not want to be a marginal figure in his family's life.

Urged to think about skills and talents that he had no time to enjoy anymore, Alex recalled that he had once enjoyed gardening and told Joe that he had started life as a carpenter/builder, which meant that he had expert practical skills that he no longer made much use of.

Through relaxation and guided imagery, Joe encouraged Alex to see how the future might go, if he didn't address his work addiction. Jane would want a divorce and he would have to leave the family home. With finances as they were, he would be lucky to afford a badly furnished bedsit for himself and he would see even less of his children than he did now. Jane had always had wholesome meals ready for him, even at the typically late hour that he would arrive home from work. Left to himself, he would probably grab junk-food snacks, if he remembered to eat at all, and his health would quickly suffer. If he became ill, no one would be able to take over the running of the firm, as he had never been willing to delegate key responsibilities, so no one would know what to do. He might end up losing everything.

Then Alex was asked to imagine how his life might be better if he did not spend every possible hour at work. He could revitalise his relationship with his wife and re-start activities they had used to enjoy together, such as country walks and theatre going. He could develop a real, loving relationship with his children and take his two sons fishing or play football with them. There would be time to visit wider family again. He would be a nicer person to live with and he would like himself better. If he re-thought his business plans more realistically and scaled down his commitments, his business could still prosper. He visualised himself experiencing this more satisfying lifestyle.

Joe also helped Alex to see how he had fallen into the trap of all-or-nothing, emotional thinking. Alex believed that, because he wasn't currently highly successful, he must be a complete failure. Once he could see that the situation was not either/or, he was able to create the mental space to think about some practical solutions to his company's difficulties, which were giving him the justification to indulge his workaholism.

As a result, he decided to ask his father for financial help. This was an enormous step forward for Alex, as he had believed that his father would only approve of him if he were self-sufficient. In fact, his father was only too willing to help. (It turned out that in later life, he too had realised that he

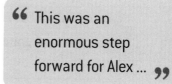

This was an enormous step forward for Alex ...

had lost out on more meaningful ways of living his life, because of his own preoccupation with work and empire building.)

Joe set Alex some tasks that led him to spend much more time with his family. These included taking back responsibility for the gardening (making it a fun activity the children could share in) and deciding on how to redecorate and refurbish the house, which was becoming sadly dilapidated. This was a joint project that he and Jane could become involved in

> **" Re-structuring his life to meet his needs, meant Alex became a far happier person. "**

together. Alex also undertook to come up with ideas for, and to arrange, some novel outings for the whole family. Meanwhile, he re-appraised his business and his management style and learned to delegate where appropriate.

The more Alex broadened his talents and shared his time with those close to him, the better he began to feel about himself. He realised that seeking to get his self-esteem entirely from his business activities was bad for all concerned. It had resulted in his setting no limits to his business ambitions. And deriving all his satisfaction from taking greater and greater risks with expansion, in the hope of greater financial and emotional gains, had, on the contrary, sapped his energy

---

What workaholism does to you

Working compulsively causes ...

- mental and physical stress
- a variety of illnesses arising from stress, such as heart disease, stomach ulcers and certain cancers
- poor nutrition, as a result of skipping meals
- a lowered immune system, leading to susceptibility to infection
- marital breakdown
- impaired relationships with family and friends.

and his confidence and distanced him from his wife and children. When he re-structured his life in a way that allowed him to meet his needs, and, just as importantly, for those involved with him to meet theirs too, in a balanced way, he became a far happier and more open-minded person.

Mitchell's false gold

Mitchell was 25 and married with a three-year-old daughter when he came to see Joe. Although he had a well-paid job in a city bank, this was now in jeopardy because of his increasing dependence on drugs. He had started with cannabis, 'chilling out' at home in the evenings, and then graduated to cocaine. He was increasingly failing to meet deadlines and had occasionally even missed important meetings. And it wasn't just work that was being affected; he was also having regular heavy rows with his wife and had started to have blackouts.

Mitchell was identifying very heavily with his life as a cocaine-user, loving the euphoria and confidence it gave him. Every weekend he went to clubs with colleagues who were single or had broken marriages. But, although he wanted to carry on with that lifestyle, he didn't want to lose his job or his marriage, and was therefore very agitated when he arrived to see Joe.

Having calmed him down, Joe encouraged Mitchell to separate himself from his cocaine use by talking about the addiction as something outside of him. He talked of how the addiction was affecting Mitchell, how the addiction was lying to him, and so on. Mitchell soon realised that he had used the addiction to help him avoid his frustration about being tied down with a young child, while still only a young man. But, although he felt frustrated, he genuinely adored his wife and daughter. When he weighed up the benefits and costs of his addiction, his fear of losing his family was greater than his fear of being trapped in a domestic lifestyle.

> 66 Mitchell soon realised that he had used the addiction to avoid his frustration ... 99

So, while Mitchell was deeply relaxed, Joe encouraged him to concentrate on the shame and self-disgust he felt about wasting his time and money on pursuing an illusion (that of being a single, carefree man) instead of spending it on improving his family's quality of life and furthering his career. With further guided imagery and visualisation, Joe then encouraged Mitchell to realise how much he could gain by kicking the habit – the return of his health, the love of his family, self-respect, respect from others, and the fantastic feeling that comes from making one's own decisions and mastering skills. He showed Mitchell how to view his family life in a positive way, and how, by working at his promising career, he could earn enough to generate many opportunities for travel and other experiences that they could all enjoy together.

What cocaine does to you

Cocaine, a white powder that is 'snorted', creates a euphoric rush that lasts for about 30 minutes and a wakefulness that persists for hours. Frequent use can lead to ...

- exhaustion, nerviness, weight loss and damage to the nasal passages (in effect, a hole where there used to be nostrils)
- severe chest pains – indeed, a significant number of cocaine users end up in accident and emergency departments, fearing they are having heart attacks
- a terrible low after the high. Many people resort to taking more, to avert the low. But the next high is never as good as the last, whereas the next low is even *more* dire than the previous one
- the brain continuing to race, long after the euphoria has worn off, preventing sleep
- irritability, depression and paranoia
- sudden and strong sexual cravings, leading to often irresponsible sexual behaviours
- debt and crime. Cocaine is extremely costly, leading people into theft and prostitution to feed their habit.

Crack cocaine (crystals like small yellow, pink or whitish rocks, which are smoked) creates an instant intense high but one that lasts just minutes. After only a few weeks of use, people become aggressive, violent and suspicious even of their own friends and families. They suffer delusions, lose their sense of judgement and, increasingly, their contact with reality. Sometimes crack use can even lead to death from respiratory failure or heart disease. Feeding a crack habit can easily cost about £200 a day.

Amphetamines (speed) are often known as the poor man's cocaine. They speed up the nervous system, increasing energy and movement. Users may speak very quickly and their thoughts may run ahead of them. Coming down may be accompanied by exhaustion and depression.

Knowing the power of metaphor, Joe also told him a story about a merchant who made a good living selling cloth. One day a woman came to see him, asking him to match some material that she had a roll of, and the merchant realised, with shock, that in amongst its many colours it contained pure gold

What cannabis does to you

Cannabis takes the form of dried leaves usually smoked in a cigarette or 'joint'. Users may say it brings on feelings or euphoria of relaxation or that it makes them feel more comfortable and sociable. But regular cannabis use is linked with ...

- depression and increased risk of psychosis

- a massive increase in the risk of developing schizophrenia

- paranoia and memory loss

- lethargy and apathy – in effect, knocking out all motivation. Long-term use negatively affects intellectual abilities, careers and social life – and *reduces* life satisfaction rather than increasing it

- distorted perceptual judgements. This effect lasts long after the 'high' has worn off. A significant proportion of car accidents are linked with cannabis use and, increasingly, injuries involving industrial equipment

- cancers. Smoking joints is an even bigger cancer risk than smoking cigarettes

- increased risk of acute and chronic bronchitis, affecting quality of life

- increased appetite, so may lead to undesired weight gain.

thread. The woman had no idea of its value, so, suddenly greedy to have it, he told her that it couldn't be matched. He told her that, as so little would be no good for her purposes and as he was a kind-hearted fellow, he would buy the material from her and sell it for scrap. The woman agreed to this.

The merchant had always been a kindly, honest man but, once he was in possession of the gold-thread material, he became a different person. Every day, instead of concentrating on his work, the merchant shut up shop early and spent long hours painstakingly unpicking the gold thread, planning to sell it for a huge profit. He neglected his wife and his responsibilities in his urgency to earn a fortune. As he worked, he imagined how he would spend his gains on himself, travelling to parts of the world he had never seen, to look for ever more exotic cloths. With his new-found riches, he might even find himself a new glamorous wife, instead of the one he had, who nowadays just seemed to complain incessantly about his absence.

Eventually the task was complete. He had mound upon mound of the sparkling gold thread. The moment had come to melt it down into solid gold! He read up everything he needed to know about how to do it, acquired the right utensils and began. But alack, to his horror the thread turned black and soon frazzled to nothing.

His wife came into the shop and found him inconsolable, although she didn't know what had happened. And, despite the fact that he had neglected her and their needs for some considerable time, she did everything she could to raise his spirits, reassuring him of her love and encouraging him to believe in himself as a good and talented man. It was then that the merchant realised that he had been the victim of greed, led astray by an illusion, and that he already had true gold right where he lived. This story resonated with Mitchell at a deep level, helping to reinforce his desire to live a meaningful life.

He agreed to think about his worst-case scenario and all the downsides of cocaine (see the box on page 189) whenever he was tempted to go clubbing with his friends. He would concentrate on specific work goals and arrange weekend trips and treats, which he could enjoy with his wife and daughter – as well as finding a way for him and his wife to have the occasional weekend away alone together. He also decided to plan a dream holiday with his wife and put money away to save for it.

Mitchell needed to see Joe just three times, mainly to keep him motivated and to talk through any problems.

Jeanette's bereavement

Jeanette, a part-time teacher, was just 52 when her husband died suddenly. They had had almost 30 years of happy marriage together. As Jeanette had always had a drink or two socially, it was quite natural for her to think of having a couple of glasses of wine at night, after her husband's death, to dull the pain of her loneliness and sadness a little, and perhaps help her sleep. She had never kept wine in the house before, but now there was always a bottle in the fridge. Over a period of a year, her drinking escalated dramatically. Quite quickly, she found she was drinking three or four glasses a night, then a whole bottle. Soon wine wasn't strong enough and she was drinking a bottle of sherry a night.

When neighbours or friends from work rang to invite her around or suggest some activity to get her out of the house, she found excuses, as she couldn't face the thought of not having her drink and she didn't want anyone to know how dependent on it she had become. As a consequence, she became more and more lonely. Soon, she was experiencing monumental hangovers in the mornings and was also obliged to take a small bottle of vodka into work with her because a nip of it now and then was the best way to deal with the hangovers. But her image of herself as a kind and caring person no longer fitted with the present reality – a selfish drunk, as she described herself. She also loved her grown-up son and his family dearly and didn't want to lose them.

One night her son had called round unexpectedly and found her in the kitchen, blind drunk. They had had a major row and he stormed out, shouting angrily that, unless she got herself some help, he wouldn't want to see her any more, or let her see his two young sons. Jeanette had had such a shock when he threatened to abandon her and prevent her from seeing her grandchildren, that she was three-quarters resolved to stop drinking before she walked into the therapy room. Joe's job was to strengthen her resolve, and help her recover her old sense of self, so that she could find ways to deal with the loneliness that had precipitated her slump into alcoholism.

Joe praised Jeanette for her skill in building and maintaining relationships, as she had kept her marriage happy for 30 years and clearly had friends and colleagues who cared about her. She was also a popular teacher. Then he encouraged her to express her worst fears. Immediately Jeanette answered that her worst nightmare would be to get caught with drink at work. She would lose her job. With nothing left to live for, she would no doubt drink even more heavily and her son would definitely disown her.

So next Joe relaxed Jeanette and encouraged her to visualise herself in this worst scenario – to feel the shame of being caught in the act of drinking at work and picture the terrible consequence of losing her job. "Visualise yourself sick and alone. You've lost your family now, as well as your job. Neighbours ignore you. You are dependent on benefits, not eating properly and not heating your home, because you need to spend what money you have on drink. You are miserable, lonely and ashamed. No one respects you. All those dreams you had, of things you wanted to show your grandchildren, are never going to come true. You are starting to find you can't remember things you've done and keep repeating yourself. Once you forgot your own name ..."

While she was still relaxed, he then encouraged her to visualise her life as she would like it to be. Jeanette had decided that her goals were to be able to enjoy a social drink and to find meaningful ways to fill her excess leisure time. She didn't want to stop drinking completely, because she had always enjoyed a drink when having dinner with friends and considered it part of being sociable. She planned not to drink when alone, however, and never to have alcohol in the house,

> **❝ One of her goals was to still be able to enjoy a drink socially ... ❞**

unless guests were coming, in which case she would provide just wine. She visualised herself spending happy times with her son and family, entertaining her friends and using her free time working at a charity shop and studying again.

When she next saw Joe, she told him she had arranged to become a volunteer at a local charity shop, on a day that she

> **Jeanette has had no further problem with addiction ...**

wasn't at school. She had made contact again with the friends whom she had abandoned, and suggested get-togethers. She had also decided to study for an MA in the field of education, which would involve her in visiting other schools and looking at good practice.

She told Joe, "I will never stop missing my darling husband but I'm ready to make something of my own life again." Jeanette has had no further problems with addiction.

Craig's chatline 'habit'

Craig's secret phone sex-life was suddenly discovered by his furious wife Meryl, when she checked through their itemised phone bill and found a large number of calls had been made to premium rate numbers. She was so devastated when she discovered that he had been listening and masturbating while on the phone to different girls that she threatened to end their relationship and take their baby twins with her, unless he sought instant help.

When Craig subsequently saw Ivan, he was confused about why he had been ringing the sex chatlines. But, after some discussion, it emerged that arguments seemed to be the common trigger. His usual response to any major argument was to close up, go and lock himself in his den, and ring a sex line. Having phone sex helped him discharge his pent-up feelings.

When Craig spoke of his reaction to arguments, it was clear that he had very strong feelings about them. Through gentle probing, Ivan found out that, many times as a young child, Craig had clung terrified to the upstairs banisters, listening to his parents arguing furiously below, throwing pans or even chairs at each other. His mother was regularly beaten and sometimes Craig was hit too. Although his father had left home when Craig was 10, never to be in contact again, Craig had already learnt from the whole shattering experience that disagreements always escalated into anger and violence, and were to be avoided at all costs.

Ivan helped him to recognise that there are conflicts in all relationships and that what he needed to do was to learn more effective ways to manage them when they arose. One of these was to learn how to listen (without interruption) and how to negotiate (taking turns to speak, being specific about one's own wants while also acknowledging the other person's position, not hurling personal insults, not bringing up past misdemeanours and so on). If Craig's emotional arousal became too high, Ivan suggested, he should take time out, for instance by going for a walk, and then come back later, having calmed down again, to continue listening and negotiating.

> **66** He used phone sex to discharge his pent-up feelings. **99**

Ivan also used the rewind technique with Craig, a simple,

How the rewind technique works

THE REWIND technique should be carried out by an experienced practitioner. It is performed when you are in a state of deep relaxation. Once relaxed, you are asked to recall or imagine a place where you feel totally safe and at ease, much as in the way we suggested in "Create a special, peaceful place" on page 133. Your relaxed state is then deepened. You are then asked to imagine that, in your special place, you have a TV set and a video player with a remote control facility. Next, you are asked to float to one side of yourself, out of your body, and watch yourself watching the screen, without actually seeing the picture. (This is a means of creating significant emotional distance.)

You next watch yourself watching a 'film' of the traumatic event, the memory of which is still adversely affecting you today. The film begins at a point before the trauma occurred and ends at a point at which the trauma is over and you feel safe again. In your imagination, you then float back into your body and imagine pressing the video rewind button, so that you see yourself very quickly going backwards through the trauma, from safe point to safe point. Then you watch the same images, but going forwards very quickly, as if pressing the fast forward button.

All this is repeated back and forth, at whatever speed feels comfortable, and as many times as you need, till the scenes evoke no emotion. If the feared circumstance is one that you will confront again in the future – for instance, driving a car ▶

effective means of removing the emotional power from traumatising memories (see "How the rewind technique works" opposite). This meant that Craig could stop pattern matching to memories of fights and violence at home during his childhood whenever he and Meryl had disagreements. Afterwards, while Craig was still in a deeply relaxed state, Ivan invited him to imagine himself having a disagreement with Meryl in the future, but this time seeing himself discussing the matter sensibly with her, and with both of them listening to each other and negotiating calmly – the shared aim being to reach a satisfactory solution for both of them.

Craig was also worried about the financial responsibilities of supporting a wife and young twins, although he earned a good living as a self-employed plumber. He worried about what would happen if work stopped coming in or his wife

or using a lift – you are asked to imagine a scenario in which you are feeling confident and relaxed while doing so. After this, the work of the rewind technique is complete.

Besides being safe, quick and painless, the technique has the advantage of being non-voyeuristic. Intimate details do not have to be made public. It is you who watches the 'film', not the therapist. ●

A full explanation of this technique can be found in our book, Human Givens: A new approach to emotional health and clear thinking. *It is a highly effective way of dealing with post traumatic stress or phobias.*

got pregnant again. Ringing the sex lines, he said, helped him to put all his concerns out of his mind (conveniently forgetting the prohibitive, mounting cost of the phone calls themselves, although he worried about this later). Ivan showed Craig how he was grossly misusing his imagination to invent scenarios

> 66 ... having learnt to handle his fear of arguments, he had no more wish to pursue his addiction. 99

that had no especial likelihood of occurring. Work was plentiful and increasing, and Meryl was using contraception.

Praising Craig, however, for the power of his imagination, Ivan encouraged him to put it to better use, by imagining a realistic and positive future for himself and his family. He had little difficulty in helping Craig feel disgust about his impulsive use of the sex chatlines or in building on his fear of losing Meryl and the children. Then he encouraged Craig to recall the passionate sex life he and Meryl had used to enjoy before the arguments between them had escalated, as well as his delight in spending time with the twins.

Once Craig had learned to handle his fear of arguments, he had no more wish to pursue his addiction. He decided to spend the money he saved from not phoning the sex lines on taking his wife out to dinner once a week.

Craig needed to see Ivan just the once.

"Respect, man, innit"

Harry, at 18, was a heroin addict. He went to see Pamela because he wanted to change his life – he was sick of feeling so low when he came off his heroin highs and of having no money. When Pamela asked about his interests in life, his face lit up when he told her how he loved playing and mixing his decks and that he had even been a DJ in a few clubs, but, he said, sometimes the drugs stopped him.

After relaxing Harry deeply, Pamela asked him to think, with his eyes closed, about both sides of his life: Harry the talented deck-mixer and Harry the drug abuser. She asked him to visualise himself standing in the centre of a long horizontal pole and, in his imagination, to walk to one end, where his drug life was. "Really see it, smell it and touch it," she said. ("It was vile," he told her afterwards.) Then she asked him to walk back to the middle, and then on to the other end of the pole to see that aspect of his life for what it really meant to him – enjoyment, achievement, freedom, money. Again she asked him to really focus on these things.

Pamela had Harry repeat this several times, still in his relaxed state, with the length of the pole gradually shortening and the ends coming in closer and closer to the middle. Finally, for one very brief moment, she asked him to bring both sides inside himself and urged, "Make your choice – *now!*"

"Life! I choose life!" cried out Harry. He was strongly affected by this experience and, when he came back for another session, four weeks later, he told Pamela he hadn't taken drugs at all. However, he had still found himself wanting heroin on occasions and he had also been drinking heavily.

What heroin does to you

Heroin, an opiate that comes from the poppy plant, comes in the form of a white powder that is injected or smoked. It creates a rush of euphoria or pleasure and may make people feel detached from their worries or events. However, the downside is much greater. Heroin causes ...

- slowed heart rate and sluggish breathing – which is what causes death after overdose
- constipation and difficulty passing urine
- ejaculation problems and sterility
- menstrual disturbances
- heightened susceptibility to infections because of effects on the immune system
- severe irritation of the skin, leading to fevered scratching
- amnesia
- teeth and hair to fall out, after long-term use
- increased risk of hepatitis and HIV from shared needles
- a confidence that can take the form of arrogance and aggressiveness
- detachment from pain or injury – you know you've hurt yourself, perhaps badly, but you don't care.

Now he wanted to be able to stop both. This motivation had been reinforced by the fact that he had had some really brilliant nights when he had realised just how talented he was with his mixing.

When Pamela asked him what he expected from drugs and drinking, he said it was the excitement and adrenalin rush he was after, but he had also realised that he didn't actually get it. He *had*, however, got a high from mixing and 'being clean'. So, making use of the fact that the floor represented a comfort zone to Harry – she knew that he would always sort out his DVDs and discs on the floor – Pamela suggested they get down on the floor to do a drawing of the brain.

> 66 He got a natural high from 'being clean'. 99

She asked him what he thought the boss's secretary (the anterior cingulate) would look like, and he said, "A girl of about 16". He saw himself as the boss. Suddenly he realised that he – a man, as he saw himself – was being controlled by a young girl and not only that but he was paying her all his money to let him do things that weren't in his best interest! It became clear that, in his world, he expected to look after girls, not have rings run round him by them.

Pamela then showed him the cunning way that the young secretary was sprinkling on her own dusting of dopamine to make him want to take drugs – and that it was *her* urge, not his. "You could get her to sprinkle on the dopamine while you are playing your decks, and not pay her anything at all!" said Pamela. This was an extremely powerful image to Harry.

Pamela reminded him of all his good experiences and of how these were now set up in his hippocampus – which he chose to think of as a new stack of DVDs in his disc collection.

When he came back six weeks later, he was able to report that he had been doing some deck mixing, smoking just the occasional cigarette and drinking Pepsi. He has now gone to college to take a music technician course. His parting words to Pamela were, "Respect, man, innit".

Gambling

There is an upward trend in the number of people who gamble, with over half the population involved in at least one gambling activity each week – albeit much of it relatively harmless fun like doing the lottery. However, between one and two per cent of the adult population develop a serious addiction to gambling, which can lead to:

- behaviour which is progressively out of control and compulsive
- obsessing about raising more money to gamble
- illegal behaviour, such as stealing, to fund it
- continual fantasising about gambling
- adverse effects on relationships
- adverse effects on ability to function in society.

Gambling it all away

Brian, a 32-year-old London civil servant went to see Ivan because his wife, Wendy, was threatening to leave him. They had been married for eight years and had two children. Wendy had returned to work and was now in a successful role with exciting prospects that were a constant talking point among their relatives and friends.

It quickly became apparent, however, that the reason Wendy was talking about leaving was that she was frightened by Brian's excessive gambling. As a young man Brian got a buzz from fruit machines but later he fell heavily into betting on the horses. Now his gambling was accelerating out of all control. It had got so bad that Wendy had been put in the humiliating position of having to borrow money from her mother to pay household bills that *he* was supposed to pay. The crisis that precipitated her threat to leave was the discovery that he had also built up considerable debts on credit cards that he had concealed from her. His behaviour was undermining *her* need for security.

Ivan found that Brian had two important needs not being met. He was unfulfilled by his work in a career that did not stretch him and his need for status was constantly being undermined by his wife's successful career advancements. Brian sought an escape from this unhappiness in the buzz induced by gambling, which seemed more real and thrilling to him than ordinary life.

Further investigation revealed that what he really wanted to do in his life was train as a solicitor, but he lacked the confidence to do so. Using guided imagery, Ivan helped him to make a more realistic assessment of his ability levels. At Brian's second session, a month later, he gleefully reported that his employer was willing to support him in starting training for a career as a solicitor. He then no longer needed the false buzz and illusion of power that gambling had brought him. Six months later he contacted Ivan to say that he was getting genuine satisfaction and a renewed sense of status from working to build a career that truly stretched him. He had stopped gambling; his wife had given him her full support for his new direction and life looked better than he had ever thought possible.

> 66 He had stopped gambling and life looked better than he had ever thought possible. 99

Oscar quits smoking at last

Oscar was a middle-aged man whose wife had walked out on him many years before, leaving him to bring up their two children. Although he had started to drink too much for a while, he had managed to cut down again to sensible levels without any help, realising that he did not want to risk having his children taken from him. However, he just could not kick the habit of smoking. He would stop for a while and then lapse, as regularly as clockwork.

Whenever he lapsed he would come to see Joe, to help him get back on track. After this had happened a few times, Joe said, "Oscar, can you not see a pattern to these lapses?"

"A pattern?" said Oscar.

"Yes. When do these lapses tend to occur?"

"Oh, there's no pattern," said Oscar. "Look at what happened this time. I was at a wedding, having a good time, and my brother-in-law was smoking and it just looked so tempting, so I had one with my drink. But last time, I wasn't drinking. It was just after my football team won a fantastic victory – I was there watching. And the time before, let me see, oh yes, it was when my son graduated from university with his degree and I went to the ceremony. I don't know why but I had a cigarette outside, afterwards, when the photographs were being taken."

"Of course there's a pattern there, Oscar!" said Joe. "You lapse when you're celebrating! When you are extra happy, your guard goes down. What you need to do is recognise that celebrations are high-risk situations for you. You need to imprint firmly in your mind beforehand the negatives of giving in and the positives of staying off. Think how you will feel about yourself if you give in and the next day you wake up with a sore throat, your hair stinking of smoke and you're back to smoking 40 cigarettes a day again. Think about worrying about the threat of lung cancer and heart attacks and dying too young and leaving your children with no one to look after them. You wouldn't want them to go through all

Smoking can cause ...

- lung cancer – 90 per cent of lung cancers occur in smokers
- heart disease – a third of all deaths from heart disease and 80 per cent of heart attacks suffered by smokers in early middle age are smoking-induced. Ultrasound studies show thickening of the arteries, which can lead to heart attacks, even in teenage and young adult smokers
- cancers of the lip, mouth, pharynx, larynx, oesophagus, pancreas and bladder
- cancer of the cervix
- the loss of legs and arms – over 2000 amputations of limbs are performed each year, because of peripheral vascular disease (seriously obstructed circulation), mainly caused by smoking
- bronchitis, emphysema and other respiratory diseases, which are often highly disabling, affecting ability to walk or do any physical activities
- urinary incontinence in women and breast abscesses that are not due to breastfeeding
- backache
- wrinkling and sallowness of the skin
- loss of teeth
- stomach ulcers.

that extra suffering, would you, after you did so much to help them get over losing their mother?

"Think about how good you will feel if you say no, and the next day you wake up feeling great. You'll have enjoyed the celebration just the same amount, whichever one you do.

> **66** That was enough to help him stay off cigarettes for good. **99**

"If you need extra help, instead of coming to see me *after* a celebration, come to me beforehand, and together we'll rehearse the strategy that will keep you off smoking, rather than getting back on track!"

That was enough to help Oscar stay off cigarettes for good.

You don't have to settle for false gold

We hope you have found this book helpful and that it has given you the information and encouragement you need to overcome your own problematic activity successfully. As you have seen, it *is* possible to beat addiction, if you truly want to, and with the minimum of discomfort. But don't worry if you find that you relapse – simply use the extra information this gives you about your own personal situation to help you succeed in the future.

Remember, addiction tricks us – it is false gold, an illusion that will never live up to its promise. It can be a difficult adversary but, as it is no cleverer than you are, you are

> **As you have seen, it *is* possible to beat addiction.**

certainly more than a match for it. So, whether you need a helping hand to start you off or not, you now have all the information you need, and the know-how, to take back control of your life.

A sense of control over our lives is worth fighting for. It's one of our basic needs – a human given.

* * * * *

INDEX

If you have found this book helpful, you might
like to recommend it to friends or colleagues
who could benefit from reading it too.

It's available through all good book shops or
direct from HG Publishing on 01323 811662
or online at: www.humangivens.com

How to lift depression... *fast*

"An empowering book ... immediately useful ... Read, use, enjoy and reap the benefits for yourself and others." *Ruth Morozzo, 'Footnotes' Journal*

"As a GP I see many people suffering from depression, and have searched for many years for a good book to recommend to them. At last I have found one. This book draws together the most effective methods from many different approaches to treatment, yet is written in a style which makes the ideas easy to understand and put into practice. The 'human givens' approach detailed in this book is a major step forward in helping people suffering from depression and other mental health problems." *Dr Gina Johnson*

"At last some concrete practical advice. This book offers some real solutions and insight into depression. I can't recommend it enough. If you are suffering from depression or you are caring or treating anyone with this condition, this book will be indispensible. I have spent a lot of money and time researching depression and can say this is without doubt the best book I have read on the subject – I urge you to buy it." *Amazon Review*

"This book is the first I have come across on the subject of depression that is easy to read and understand for both professionals and lay people. It will prove an invaluable resource... The title cover carries the phrase 'Change is much easier than you think' and that theme flows throughout the book. [It] offers readers much practical help and advice ... a book for every library and one that should not sit on the shelf and gather dust." *'Professional Social Work' Magazine*

"Everyone involved in administering personal therapy should read this book." *Nursing Standard*

How to lift depression... fast is published in paperback
by HG Publishing (2005) ISBN: 1-899398-414

Human Givens:
A new approach to emotional health and clear thinking

"An entirely attainable and reasonable road map for good mental health." *Irish Examiner*

"In *Human Givens* Griffin and Tyrrell offer innovative perspectives on promoting effective living. They have synthesized brain and social research in such a way that they provide new templates for understanding how to unlock the best in human nature." *Dr Jeffrey K. Zeig, Director of the Milton H. Erickson Foundation*

"A quiet revolution." *New Scientist*

"Big idea... Key insight... Weekly excavation of your painful past in an attempt to understand your present depression has never seemed so foolish." *Financial Times*

"Harnessed between these pages are scientific insights and practical techniques of sufficient power to completely revolutionise our approach to parenting, teaching and the caring professions. I wholeheartedly recommend *Human Givens* to any individual with a burning interest in how life works and can be helped to work better."
Dr Nick Baylis, Lecturer in Positive Psychology, Cambridge University

"Real breakthroughs in the behavioural sciences are rare, and it's smart to beware of hype. But not all scientific progress is incremental. Sometimes, as in the germ theory of disease, it's exponential. Griffin and Tyrrell's contribution advances psychology as much as the introduction of the Arabic numeric system with its zero digit advanced mathematics." *Washington Times*

"While books are never a cure for what ails us in life, they are often a catalyst, a trigger that fires off those rare and profound 'aha!' moments that lead to deeper insights and understanding. *Human Givens* is such a catalyst." *Jack Davies*

"[This] approach offers a refreshing alternative to reams of expensive psychobabble." *The Big Issue*

"Important original work ... both aesthetically pleasing and of immense practical use... has great relevance to all areas of life... could save (tax payers) millions of pounds. A remarkable achievement which should attract the attention of any truly curious human being."

Dr Farouk Okhai, Consultant Psychiatrist in Psychotherapy

"*Human Givens* is the most practical and intuitive book I've read in years. People have been speculating about the utility of dreams for decades, but I think you guys have it hammered."

Charles Hayes, Autodidactic Press, USA

"A wonderfully fresh and stimulating view of dreaming, evolution, and human functioning. *Human Givens* also provides both an encompassing model and practical, specific applications to enhance the effectiveness of psychotherapy. It will deepen and widen every reader's perspective."

Arthur J. Deikman, M.D., Clinical Professor of Psychiatry, University of California

"Psychology doesn't have to be difficult and mystique has no part especially when the writers cross boundaries to take from all quarters and from there synthesize with such clarity. Some purists may not like it [*Human Givens*] but broken fences facilitate a wider view and allow one to see further." *Leo Kingdon*

Human Givens: A new approach
to emotional health and clear thinking
by Joe Griffin and Ivan Tyrrell

Published in paperback by HG Publishing (2004) ISBN: 1-899398-317

Dreaming Reality:
How dreaming keeps us sane, or can drive us mad

"*Dreaming Reality* exquisitely scythes through the Gordian knot created by past dream theories. Even better, like all the very best explanations, its central theme is as far-reaching as it is intuitive. Through a fascinating combination of dream examples and scientific findings, it provides lucid and compelling evidence for how our night and daydreams not only mould our personalities but also lie at the very heart of being human." *Dr Clive Bromhall, author of 'The Eternal Child'*

"A remarkable book that makes compelling reading. Griffin and Tyrrell's adriotly written text challenges traditional views on our knowledge and understanding of the mystifying covert world of dreams." *Professor Tony Charlton, Professor of behavioural studies, University of Gloucestershire*

"This book is revolutionary in more than one way. Past and sometimes overlooked research is re-evaluated, and a persuasive theory emerges... long overdue to my mind." *Doris Lessing*

"For anyone who has speculated on the meaning and purpose of dreaming, Griffin and Tyrrell's astounding insights light up the dark corners of the mind. Not since 1964 when Carl Jung's book *Man and his Symbols* was published has anyone set out to write so conclusively on dreaming for a wide audience.

Griffin and Tyrrell [propose] that dreaming functions to cleanse the undischarged emotional arousals of the day and they explain how this happens through metaphorical pattern-matching. From this one sets off on the journey to understanding the true causes of (and routes to healing) depression.

This book is revolutionary in thought, revelatory in content and will be established as the most important twenty-first century milestone on the road to accessible mental health treatment for all. It's a must for all who live with mental illness or work for its relief." *Ian Hunter* OBE

Dreaming Reality: How dreaming keeps us sane, or can drive us mad is published in hardback by HG Publishing (2004) ISBN: 1-899398-368